Santa Clara County
LIBRARY

Renewals:
(800) 471-0991
www.santaclaracountylib.org

:s 2

DISCOVER CALIFORNIA SHRUBS

MaryRuth Casebeer

Illustrated by Peggy Edwards-Carkeet

HOOKER PRESS

Although the author and publisher have made every effort to ensure the accuracy and completeness of information contained in this book, we assume no responsibility for errors, inaccuracies, omissions, or any inconsistency herein. Any slights of people, places, or organizations are unintentional.

ISBN: 0-9665463-1-8
Library of Congress Control Number: 2003-101573

Map adapted from Hoover et al., revised by Douglas E. Kyle
Historic Spots in California
Copyright © 1932, 1933, 1937, 1948, 1966, 1990 by the Board of Trustees of the Leland Stanford Junior University.
With the permission of Stanford University Press, www.sup.org.

Front cover photo copyright © 2004 by Patrick Stone.
Background photo by MaryRuth Casebeer
Black and white illustrations copyright © 2004
by Peggy Edwards-Carkeet.
Colored illustrations copyright © 2004 by Peggy Edwards.

Front cover photo: *Ribes speciosum,* Fuchsia-Flowered Gooseberry
Background photo: *Arctostaphylas patula,* Greenleaf Manzanita

For Kalen, another Blazing Star; and Olivia and Diego, the youngest Woodland Stars; and all the children who will learn to love, treasure and nurture the irreplaceable native plants of California.

The author wishes to thank several people who contributed their considerable expertise to the successful completion of this book. Thanks to David Self for his careful and extremely helpful editing; to Susanne Nelson for editing the final draft and making pertinent suggestions for accuracy and clarification, and for her computer and graphic art skills; to the illustrator, Peggy Edwards-Carkeet, a longtime wildflower friend and fellow CNPS member, for her accurate and handsome shrub illustrations; and to Patrick Stone, another wildflower friend and fellow CNPS member, for sharing his invaluable native plant knowledge and beautiful California wildflower photographs.

Cover design and book production by
Dave Bonnot/Columbine Designs.
Printed on recycled, acid-free paper.

To order additional copies of *Discover California Shrubs*
from the publisher, write:

Hooker Press
P.O. Box 3957
Sonora, CA 95370-3957
Or call (800) 696-5997

Or use the order form in the back of the book.

Inclusion in this book of the many uses that Native Californians made of the native shrubs **in no way** endorses the use of any of these plants either for food or medicine by the reading public. The author and publisher accept no responsibility for any ill (deleterious) effects resulting from the use or misuse of same.

ABOUT THE AUTHOR

A resident of California for over 50 years, MaryRuth Casebeer has had a longtime love of the California flora. She has been a member of the California Native Plant Society (CNPS) for over 25 years and is a charter member of the Sierra Foothills Chapter of CNPS.

In addition to receiving a B.S. and M.S. in Nutrition from the University of California, Berkeley, MaryRuth earned a certificate in Horticulture and Landscape Design from Merritt College in Oakland, where she studied both California native and exotic plants. While attending numerous workshops, she learned about many uses the Native Californians made of native plants for food, medicine, basketmaking and more.

Over the years MaryRuth has enjoyed sharing her knowledge of native plants with young people. After retiring as a nutritionist, she organized and implemented the Project Wild Environmental Education program, in conjunction with Senior-Youth Partnership, at Curtis Creek Elementary School near Standard, California. Accompanying students on field trips, she introduced them to the wonders of the plant world outside their "back door"; establishing a school garden, she shared the magic involved in growing plants from seeds, cuttings and divisions.

MaryRuth wrote many articles about California native plants included in the CNPS Chapter booklets, *Speaking for the Plants,* Vols. I and II. In addition, she has written articles on native plants for the local newspaper, *The Union Democrat.* In her previous book, *Discover California Wildflowers*, MaryRuth presents an in-depth study of 47 native wildflowers, describing many of their unique features.

MaryRuth lives near Sonora, California, amidst the foothill natives and within an hour's drive of some of the most extraordinary wildflower "gardens" in California.

ABOUT THE ILLUSTRATOR

A native of the Central Coast of California, Peggy Edwards-Carkeet earned a B.S. in Environmental Studies from the University of California, Berkeley, and a graduate degree in Science Illustration, from the University of California, Santa Cruz.

As a natural science illustrator, and owner of Sierra Nature Prints, Peggy has serviced clients such as Calaveras Big Trees State Park, The Yosemite Association, The Sierra Club, The Nature Conservancy, and the California Department of Fish and Game. Her favorite subjects to illustrate are California native plants and insects, using techniques such as pen and ink, scratchboard, and colored pencil. She is a member of the American Association of Botanical Artists and the California Native Plant Society.

Peggy was awarded first place, Trail Guide Category, from the National Association of Interpretation, and has displayed her artwork in the Oakland Museum of California's "California Species" show as well as throughout California.

Peggy divides her time between the Central Sierra and the "inland marine sandhills" of the Central Coast of California.

Illustrations were drawn from personal slides or from sketches made in the field, using pen and ink.

FLOWER PARTS

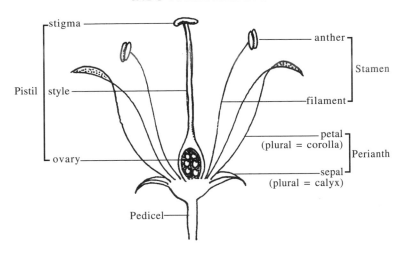

FLOWER ARRANGEMENT ON STEMS

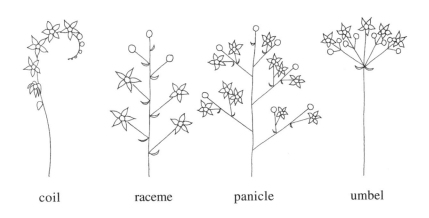

coil raceme panicle umbel

TWIG OF SHRUB

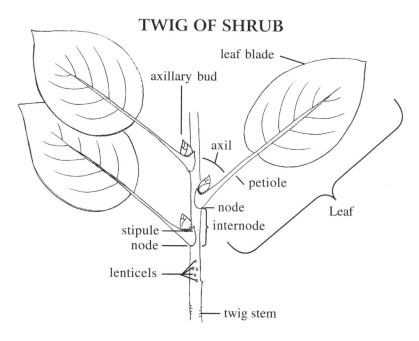

leaf blade

axillary bud

axil

petiole

node

internode

Leaf

stipule

node

lenticels

twig stem

LEAF SHAPES AND LEAF MARGINS

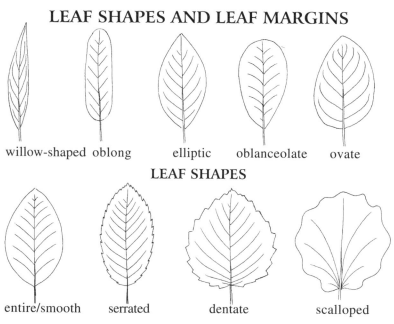

willow-shaped oblong elliptic oblanceolate ovate

LEAF SHAPES

entire/smooth serrated dentate scalloped

LEAF MARGINS

LEAF ARANGEMENT ON STEMS

alternate
sessile

alternate
with
petioles

opposite
sessile

opposite
with
petioles

SIMPLE LEAVES

lobed pinnate

lobed palmate

COMPOUND LEAVES

1-pinnate compound

palmate compound

2-pinnate
compound

even-pinnate
compound

odd-pinnate
compound

MAP OF CALIFORNIA COUNTIES

CONTENTS

INTRODUCTION

While the beauty and attractiveness of a shrub may capture our attention from a distance, only with keen and close observation do we become intimately attached to and excited about its individual charm.

California, An Island Bounded by Mountains

California is often pictured as an island—separated from adjoining states and Baja California by mountains: the Klamaths and Cascades of the north, the Sierra Nevada in the east and the San Gabriel, San Bernardino and San Jacinto mountains in the south. Both in northwestern and central western California, the Outer and Inner Coast Ranges rise abruptly behind the narrow Pacific coastal shoreline. California's Great Central Valley is situated between the Coast Ranges and the Sierras.

Because of the isolation created by these mountain barriers, the flora of California is unique. Of the almost 6,000 plant species found in California, over half are native to this state, and almost a third of those natives are endemic—species that do not grow naturally outside of California.

Additionally, the plants growing in California over the years have adapted to the hot, dry summers and cold, wet winters of California's mild mediterranean-type climate. This type of climate is only found in five locations worldwide: California, central Chile, the Cape region of South Africa, southwestern Australia and the Mediterranean basin. (About 2% of the world's total land area has a mediterranean-type climate.)

Shrubs and Trees

Shrubs and trees form the architectural structure of the natural landscape. Whether evergreen or deciduous, shrubs and trees always have "woody" stems or trunks. Shrubs decorate the scene with their silhouettes and variously colored leaves, flowers or fruits, while trees mostly add shade and height. However, the tallest plants in a specific habitat may be shrubs, not trees. (In fact, some habitats have no trees at all.)

The many woody stems of a shrub start to branch at or under the ground; with growth, these stems and branches form a bush-shaped plant. Unless it is severely pruned, one usually cannot walk under a shrub. (In contrast, trees are woody plants with only one main trunk and no side branches for 8 to 10 feet above the ground. One may easily walk under a mature tree.)

However, remember that there is a lot of variation in the natural world. Don't take these definitions too literally as each plant follows its own genetic code.

1

Native Shrubs in California

In many parts of the state, the native plant distribution bears some resemblance to that known before the huge influx of settlers in the early 1850s. However, much of the Great Central Valley is devoid of California native trees, shrubs and wildflowers because the plants' habitats have been altered or destroyed to make way for agriculture, industry or housing. But all is not lost. When you travel at the edge of the Great Central Valley, look toward the hills and take heart in seeing shrubs, trees and wildflowers "reappear".

Choice of Shrubs

Several plants, such as Buck Brush, Deer Brush, Sourberry, Oregon-Grape, Blue Elderberry and some Manzanitas. were selected because they can be seen growing throughout California. Their commonness may help the newcomer become familiar with some native plants immediately. Other shrubs were singled out for their unusually attractive or colorful flowers, fruit or leaves. Additionally, several shrubs were favored for their memorable flower fragrances; others were picked for the spicy or medicinal scents of their crushed twigs, bark or leaves.

Three vines were chosen: Virgin's Bower and Pipestems for their colorful blossoms and silvery fruit, and California Wild Grape for its large multicolored leaves and bunches of purple grapes in the fall.

Habitat

In order for a specific plant to succeed within its habitat, its essential needs for light, moisture/dryness, nutrients and heat/cold have to be satisfied. Knowing the plant's preferences will enable the reader to narrow the field when searching for a particular species.

For those plants requiring a minimal amount of light, the denser coniferous forests tend to screen out more sunlight than do the woodlands (with their scattered trees and filtered shade). Plants in need of full sunlight would of necessity dwell only in open places. Mountain Spiraea, Sierra Plum, Oregon-Grape and Greenleaf Manzanita tolerate rocky parts of the coniferous forest. Expect to find Toyon, Holly-leafed Cherry, Western Choke-Cherry, Western Redbud and Wild Mock Orange in the filtered shade of the woodlands.

Many other California native plants prefer moist conditions. Some plants that prefer shade near stream banks include Spicebush, Ninebark, American Dogwood, Douglas Spiraea, Blue Elderberry and Red Elderberry. Western Labrador Tea relishes boggy areas; Virgin's Bower insists on having damp feet and is at home in sunny, moist canyons. Other shrubs, such as Western Azalea, delight in sunny, wet meadows.

2

Many of California's sun-loving shrubs, intolerant of having their roots standing in water, will be found on open dry slopes, on gravelly slopes, in rocky soils, or in chaparral—each of which provides excellent drainage. Buck Brush, Mountain-Mahogany, Bush Poppy and Common Manzanita demand these conditions.

Bloom Time

A plant's bloom time is the range of weeks or months within which its blossoms may be found somewhere in California. The date that blooms first appear depends upon several factors, including elevation and northern or southern location in the state. Plants at lower elevations generally will bloom earlier in the year than those at higher altitudes; in addition, as one travels northward, blooming times will be later. The temperature (cold or hot) and the amount of moisture (due to rain or drought) in the several weeks before blossoming can also dramatically affect the appearance and duration of the flowers.

Of the shrubs included in this book, the first to flower are Pink Flowering Currant and Fuchsia-Flowered Gooseberry, both found in southern California in January. They usually finish blooming in May in northern California. The last to begin blossoming is Mountain Spiraea, which blooms in July and August.

Berries and Other Fruits

Of the 48 plants in the book, 28 have small, round or oblong fleshy fruits that are commonly called *berries*. Botanically speaking, only those fruits with the seeds mixed throughout the fleshy pulp, and with no inner core or pit, are berries. This definition applies to the fruits of Oregon-Grape, *Rhamnus* and *Ribes* species and California Wild Grape.

Fleshy fruits with seeds in an inner core (such as an apple) are called *pomes*; plants with pomes include Toyon, Service-Berry and Mountain Ash. Fleshy fruits with a stony pit enclosing the seed are called *drupes*; shrubs with these fruits include Manzanitas, American Dogwood, *Prunus* species, Sourberry, Poison Oak, Snowberry, Blue Elderberry and Red Elderberry.

In this book, shrubs with berry-like fruits will first have their fruit identified as *berries* or *pomes* or *drupes*; then, during further discussion of the fruit (size, color or use), the word "berries" will be used.

A Note on the Naming of Plants

Every plant belongs to a family and has a family name. Furthermore, each plant has both a Latin first and last name; these Latin names are used throughout the scientific world. The first name, or *genus*, is equivalent to our surname, while the last name, or *species*, corresponds to our given name. Just as there are many people with the same surname, plants may have several species in one genus. Additionally, some plants have *common names*, which are comparable to our nicknames.

Throughout the world, each genus/species has its unique characteristics. Common names, on the other hand, can apply to one or several plants. If persons want to be sure they are describing the same plant, they must use the Latin genus/species name. (Most often the genus/species names are derived from Latin words. Occasionally the names may be derived from Greek words, as is the genus name *Arctostaphylos*, for the plants commonly called Manzanitas.)

Clematis ligusticifolia, a California native and member of the Buttercup Family, is often called Virgin's Bower; it is one of over 200 species of *Clematis* found around the world. In a foreign country where we might have little knowledge of the language, we probably would not be understood if we inquired if California's Virgin's Bower grew there. However, if we asked about *Clematis ligusticifolia*, someone could find the answer. Using a botanical description of the plant, a botanist would be able to identify that plant wherever it might be growing.

Book Sections and Contents

In the text, in each plant's illustration, there is a stick figure indicating the height and width of the shrub relative to a 5 1/2-foot-tall plant lover.

In addition to information about each of the shrubs themselves, many of the uses that the Native Californians made of indigenous plants are described. (Today, with permission from public agencies to collect plants, many Native Californians continue to practice the ways of their ancestors, using material collected for food, medicine or basketmaking.)

Except for California Buckeye, the shrubs in this book are arranged more or less in order of blooming. In addition, similar plants (including plants in the same genus) are grouped together to make comparison easier and to aid in the identification of each species. Within each grouping, the shrubs that blossom earlier are described before those that flower later.

California Buckeye heads the list, not for its flowers, but for its bright green leaves which unfold in January or February. They announce that spring is almost here and that wildflowers are coming soon.

Flower, Leaf and Twig Illustrations, as well as a **Map of California,** with its counties named, appear in the front of the book. In the back of the book, there are a **Glossary** that defines botanical terms used in the book, a **Selected Bibliography** and an **Index** listing both common and scientific names of the shrubs (with scientific names shown in *italics*).

Sources Used in This Book

The scientific names and most of the common names of the shrubs reflect those appearing in *The Jepson Manual: Higher Plants of California*. Often the shrub's habitat, including elevation, preferred setting and geographical distribution, was found in *The Jepson Manual*. In the event of a discrepancy in the data from several sources, the author has used the information in *The Jepson Manual* and McMinn's *An Illustrated Manual of California Shrubs* as final authorities. The McMinn *Manual* was the source for the bloom times.

Cautions

Over thousands of years, the Native Californians developed safe uses of plants for food and medicinal purposes. They devised processing methods to reduce or eliminate the toxins contained in many food plants and they established appropriate medical dosages for effective treatment of ailments and diseases with a minimum of adverse reactions. Most of this information is not available in print.

The lay public should not use native plants for food or medicine because of the difficulties in accurately identifying native plants and in knowledgeably processing them. Furthermore, it is against the law in California to collect plants on private or public lands without written permission from the landowner or the appropriate public agencies.

Let It Be

The author hopes that native plant enthusiasts, both young and old, will take this book to the meadows, the foothills or the mountains—wherever plants are blooming—and color the drawings. This will leave the shrubs intact for the next visitor to enjoy; and the field-colored illustrations will continue to bring pleasure at home.

CALIFORNIA BUCKEYE

A distinctive western plant, California Buckeye is a survivor from prehistoric times when the summers in California and the West were wet and mild. The only *Aesculus* species native to California, *A. californica* is also endemic to California, meaning that it is confined to the geographic area of this state.

California Buckeye flourishes on dry slopes, in moist canyons or near stream banks in the Coast Ranges, the Cascade Range, the Sierra Nevada and the Tehachapis. There are also scatterings of these plants in the foothills adjacent to the Great Central Valley. Found from sea level up to 4,500 feet in elevation, Buckeye is not winter-hardy in the higher mountainous areas where late spring frosts nip the buds and young leaves.

A large shrub or small tree, California Buckeye is multi-stemmed and varies from 14 to 40 feet in height; mature plants may spread from 30 to 60 feet in width. In spring, many of the smaller shrubs, rounded in shape, dot the landscape; they look like globular green balloons. In contrast, the very large shrubs—those that are much wider than they are tall—are oval-shaped and similar in appearance to giant eggs resting on their sides with foliage draped down to the ground. In fall and winter, the smooth, grayish-white bark of Buckeye stands out as it glistens in the sunlight after a winter shower.

As a butterfly is crowded inside its chrysalis, so are the neatly-folded leaflets crowded inside the bud. Then, overnight, in early February, the fat leaf buds burst open, tearing the bud covering and transforming the plant into a canopy of bright green leaves. The oblong-shaped leaflets, each up to 6 inches long, radiate from their hand-like base with 5 or more outstretched fingers. The leaflets are united at the tip of the petiole—the stalk that attaches the leaf to the plant stem. The palmately compound leaves are arranged opposite on the stem.

From May to July, the numerous pinkish-white flowers appear in clusters at the tips of the smaller branches. These clusters, about 4 to 8 inches long and 1 1/2 to 2 inches wide, stand upright, reminding one of candles in a candelabra shining above the greenery. Each flower has 4 or 5 petals, about 1/2 inch long, and 5 sepals; the 5 to 7 stamens are tipped with bright orange anthers. To some, the flowers have a sweet fragrance; to others, the odor is foul.

From one "candle" (or cluster) of flowers, there are usually only 1 or 2 pear-shaped fruits. This is not surprising, considering that only a few of the myriads of flowers in each cluster have a pistil—the fruit-bearing

organ. The smooth, rich brown-colored capsule, 1 1/2 to 2 1/2 inches long, dangles from the tip of the branch on a limber stalk. In autumn, the fruit splits open to reveal a mahogany-brown seed. To some, this shiny seed showing through a slit in the opened nut looks similar to a deer's eye—hence the common name, Buckeye.

In the heat of early summer, the leaves turn a rust-brown, the first step in conserving water by the plant. Similar to many deciduous plants native to areas with a mediterranean-type climate (a climate characterized by winter rains and summer drought), California Buckeye sheds its leaves early, in late June to early July, to save water. The metabolism of the plant slows down, allowing the limited underground water to sustain the plant until the next rainy season returns.

All parts of this plant are considered toxic to humans. It has been reported that the pollen and nectar of Buckeye flowers, when taken to the hive by non-native honeybees, will kill the young bees. No mention was made of the effect of pollen and nectar gathered by the California native solitary bees on their young.

The Native Californians used the Buckeye nuts for food only when the acorn crop was light. The nuts were gathered in the fall and stored, unroasted, for periods of up to one year. The untreated nuts required considerable processing to remove their poison, aesculin.

To process, the nuts were broken open, soaked in water, pounded

7

into a meal and then leached in running water for ten days or more. Another method was to bake the nuts for eight to ten hours, then wash, mash and leach the meal. The leached meal spoiled easily so that each batch had to be eaten within a short time. This processing of the Buckeye nuts was more tedious and time-consuming than the method used for acorns.

A very important use of the Buckeye nuts by Native Californians was for stunning fish. Unleached, mashed nuts were added to pools of water containing fish. The poison in the meal caused the fish to float to the surface where they were easily caught by hand. (Cooking the fish rendered the poison harmless.)

Medicinally, the Buckeye leaves were used to make a tea for relieving lung congestion and varicose veins.

Bowls were fashioned from Buckeye wood by the Native Californians and the wood was used extensively for fire drills to start fires on a hearth.

Aesculus is the genus name of an Italian Oak with edible acorns. The species name, *californica*, means "of California".

Caution: All parts of this plant are considered toxic to humans.

CURRANTS AND GOOSEBERRIES

Both Currants and Gooseberries are members of the *Grossulariaceae* (or Gooseberry Family), which is composed of only one genus, *Ribes*. However, about 140 species of *Ribes* grow in North America and temperate South America.

Gooseberries differ from currants in that they have spines at the stem nodes—often 1 to 3, but sometimes up to 9. Additionally, gooseberries have bristly fruits of varying coarseness, while currants have smooth berries.

PINK FLOWERING CURRANT

From San Luis Obispo to Del Norte Counties, Pink Flowering Currant often grows on north-facing or moist canyon slopes or at the edges of forests, at elevations up to 3,300 feet.It is found along the North and Central Coasts, in the San Francisco Bay area and in the outer mountains of the North and South Coast Ranges.

Ribes sanguineum var. *glutinosum* is an erect, open-branching shrub growing up to 12 feet high. The branches are unarmed—without spines—and multi-stemmed, with brown, shreddy bark. It is drought-tolerant in coastal areas, but prefers part-shade in hot arid country.

Early in the year when the leaves and flowers have barely opened, the whole plant has a spicy, aromatic fragrance. In the early 1900s, Incense-Shrub was a common name, probably because of its unusual scent. The fragrance emitted from this plant's numerous glands is further enhanced under foggy or rainy conditions—it's a wonderful time to walk in the woods amidst the currants.

From January to May, but before the leaves emerge, drooping clusters of 15 to 40 tiny flowers appear. The 2- to 4-inch-long clusters (racemes) are borne in the leaf axil. The flowers, pale to deep pink, are tubular.

Soon after the flowers burst open, the leaf bud unfolds to reveal a crinkled, bright green, crepe-paper leaf. Each maple-like leaf has 3 to 5 palmate veins arising from the base of its 3 to 5 lobes. The terminal lobe of the leaf is wider than it is long.

Generally clustered on short twigs, the deciduous leaves are 3/4 to 2 3/4 inches wide. The irregularly-toothed leaves are more or less glabrous—without hairs—on the top side and only slightly hairy underneath. The leaves of *R. s.* var. *glutinosum* are viscid; they are covered with a sticky substance that oozes out through small pores. The leaves

9

turn to a soft yellow in late summer or early fall.

Globular and up to 1/3 inch across, the blue-black to black currants are covered with a whitish or grayish film which easily rubs off. Described by many as dry, bitter or inedible, they might also be portrayed as berries having a strong wild or gamey flavor.

The genus name, *Ribes,* is from the Arabic word "ribas", meaning "acid-tasting". The species name, *sanguineum,* means red like blood; the variety, *glutinosum,* suggests an abundance of a glandular, sticky substance (especially observed on this currant's leaves).

EVERGREEN CURRANT

Growing up to 1,000 feet in elevation, Evergreen Currant, *Ribes viburnifolium,* can be found in chaparral and in moist places in side canyons of Santa Catalina Island and in the Peninsular Range of southwest San Diego County; it also extends into Baja California.

Unlike other currants, the branches of Evergreen Currant arch horizontally—usually spreading out 5 or 6 feet, but sometimes as much as 12 feet. These wine-red stems root where the tips touch the ground. The overall height is not more than 2 or 3 feet. The stems have no nodal spines; resinous glands may be found on the young stems.

The evergreen, leathery leaves, arranged alternate on the stem, are a lustrous dark green above with a lighter green underneath. The margins or edges, of the round- to oval-shaped leaves most often are entire— neither lobed nor serrated. Additionally, the leaves, 3/4 to 1 1/2 inches long, are one-veined from their bases. (Many species of currants have leaves that are deciduous,

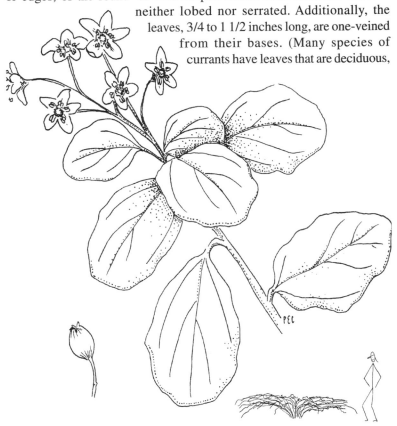

lobed and with 3 to 5 palmate veins.)

The leaf undersides are covered with yellow, resinous dots. When crushed, they exude a sweet, clean fragrance, delightful and unforgettable, and reminiscent of lemon or other citrus.

Blooming from February to April, the clusters of 6 to 15 flowers are erect and branched at the base. There are 2 or 3 clusters in each leaf axil. The individual blooms are tiny and inconspicuous, yet the brown sepals and wine-red petals occur in such abundance as to give the whole plant a reddish-maroon cast. The red fruit is globular, hairless and 1/4 inch in diameter, ripening in May.

In the California wilds, this plant is uncommon—naturally occurring only in a small area of San Diego County and on Santa Catalina Island. However, it is often seen in public and private landscaped gardens throughout the state. Because of its lustrous leaves, red stems, maroon flowers and wonderful, clean, citrusy fragrance, this handsome plant is attractive year round.

Evergreen Currant has been used extensively as a drought-tolerant ground cover under oaks and can prosper in many lower-elevation habitats if its needs are met. It requires a minimum of summer water and, if planted in clay soil in the shade, it usually needs none. During summer, in hot dry areas, Evergreen Currant desires partial-shade—morning sun only—as the leaves will scorch or turn yellow otherwise. It cannot withstand heavy frosts, so it is not a plant for the mountains.

It was first grown in England in 1897 from seed collected on Santa Catalina Island.

The genus name, *Ribes,* is from the Arabic word, "ribas", meaning "acid-tasting"; it refers to the berries. *Viburnifolium* means "having leaves similar to those of the genus *Viburnum*". This author fails to see the similarity between the leaves of the two plants, except maybe in general shape. The California native *Viburnum* is a deciduous plant; *R. viburnifolium* is evergreen, leathery and aromatic. Another common name is Santa Catalina Island Currant.

GOLDEN CURRANT

Growing up to 9,500 feet in elevation, Golden Currant is found throughout California except for the North Coast Ranges, the north coastal areas and the Mojave and Sonoran deserts. At this time, there are two varieties of *Ribes aureum* recognized in California: var. *aureum* and var. *gracillimum.*

Ribes aureum var. *aureum* grows inland in the Klamath and Cascade Ranges, the Sierra Nevada and the Great Basin. *Ribes aureum* var. *gracillimum*, growing closer to the coast, is found in the Inner North Coast Range, the San Francisco Bay area, the central and south coastal areas and the South Coast Ranges.

An erect, multi-stemmed shrub, Golden Currant may grow as high as 10 feet, but it is more commonly seen from 6 to 8 feet tall. The upright, ascending branches are smooth, as are the twigs with their gray or brown bark. The stems have no nodal spines.

The three- to five-lobed leaves are numerous on the short side twigs. Arising from the wedge-shaped leaf base, the 3 to 5 palmate leaf veins are not as prominent as those seen in many other currants.

Glandular in youth, the leathery, 3/4- to 2-inch-wide, light-green leaves are shiny and hairless when mature. Golden Currant is deciduous as are most currants. In mild climates, however, it is leafless for only a few weeks each year.

Blooming from February to June, there are 5 to 15 flowers in drooping clusters, each 1 to 2 1/2 inches long. Generally, the flowers of currants are open and bell-shaped, in contrast with those of gooseberries, which are often elongated tubes peeking out below thick foliage.

The flowers of var. *aureum* open with yellow petals that turn orange with age. Additionally, the blossoms delight us with a spicy fragrance. The blooms of var. *gracillimum* change from yellow to a deep red, but disappoint us by having no delectable scent.

The globular berries lack bristles and are hairless. About 1/4 inch in diameter, the color of the fruit may vary from red to orange to black.

Though collected by self-taught botanist John Bradbury (1768-1823) in 1810 or 1811, Thomas Nuttall (1786-1859) received credit for introducing Golden Currant to England. Later, when *Ribes aureum* was collected by Fremont on his first expedition to the West (in 1842), he referred to it as Lewis and Clark's Currant—probably found on their 1804-1806 expedition to Oregon.

Ribes, from the Arabic word "ribas", means acid-tasting; *aureum* means golden. After the long dark winter, the bright yellow and green of Golden Currant is indeed a delicious spring treat.

SIERRA GOOSEBERRY

Though it may grow up to 9,200 feet in elevation, *Ribes roezlii* is more usually seen from 3,500 to 8,500 feet in many of California's mountains: the Klamath, North Coast and Cascade Ranges; the Sierra Nevada; and the Tehachapi, Transverse and Peninsular Ranges of southern California. The most common gooseberry at mid-elevation, Sierra Gooseberry prefers coniferous forests, though it can be found in chaparral and woodlands.

A stout shrub 1 to 4 feet high, it has many long spreading branches with short rigid twigs and 1 to 3 straight spines at the stem node. Clustered on the ends of the twigs, the 1/2- to 1-inch-broad leaves are somewhat round in shape; each leaf has 3 to 5 toothed lobes and each lobe has a vein that flows from the leaf's base. The leaves are dark green above, and paler green and hairy beneath.

Blooming in June and July, the tubular flowers, in clusters of 1 to 3, are borne near the ends of the leafy twigs. The purple to dull-red sepals, each about 3/8 inch long, are reflexed, or turned back. The margins of the 5 white petals, less than half as long as the sepals, are curled inward. The anthers—the pollen-containing parts—extend well beyond the petals; the styles, attached to the pistils, protrude even further.

The red-purple or reddish berry, 1/2 to 3/4 inch in diameter, is surrounded by stout spines. Sierra Gooseberry stands out as the montane gooseberry with big bristly berries. Native Californians ate the berries after singeing the prickles in a fire. Many animals have

17

also enjoyed these gooseberries.

Ribes roezlii is an alternate host for white pine blister rust—a fungal disease accidentally introduced to the West from Europe early in the 20th Century. Though the fungus does not harm Gooseberry plants, the rust spores need a *Ribes* species host in order to develop further before they travel to nearby White or Sugar Pines. The fungus can be a serious problem for pine trees; if too many pine needles become infected and die, the whole tree will succumb to the disease.

The genus name, *Ribes*, is from the Arabic word "ribas", meaning "acid-tasting", referring to the fruit. The species, *roezlii*, is named after Bertram Roezl, son of a Czech gardener, who collected seeds in California in 1869. (He also collected seeds of Leopard Lily, Humboldt Lily and Washington Lily on that trip.)

WESTERN REDBUD

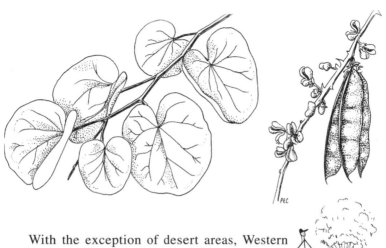

With the exception of desert areas, Western Redbud *(Cercis occidentalis)* flourishes up to 5,000 feet in elevation in all parts of California: from the North Coast, then to the Klamath, North Coast and Cascade Ranges, the Sierra Nevada and the Peninsular Ranges of southern California. It is also found in the San Joaquin Valley.

In full sun or partial shade, you will find Western Redbud in varying habitats: on dry slopes or in canyons, near stream banks, in chaparral or foothill woodlands, or on the valley floor.

Redbud appears as a stiff, upright plant with erect branches, stems and twigs. The bark on the new spring growth is reddish, maturing to a grayish-silver color. Often 6 to 15 feet tall and 8 to 10 feet wide, Redbud is usually a multi-stemmed shrub. However, it may grow up to 20 feet tall and appear tree-like. In its lower mountain range, it withstands freezing temperatures.

Like other legumes, Redbud can prosper in nitrogen-poor sandy or rocky soils because the nitrogen-fixing nodules on their roots contain bacteria that can convert nitrogen from air pockets in the soil into a form usable by the plant.

Arranged alternate on the stems, the nearly round leaves of Redbud, 2 to 3 1/2 inches wide, are heart-shaped at their bases. The margin of the leaves is entire—without teeth or scallops. Both surfaces of the leaf are shiny and glabrous.

The leaves of this shrub are simple, though many other members of the Pea or Legume Family have compound leaves with numerous pinnate or palmate leaflets. Redbud leaves are palmately-veined, each with 7 to 9 veins, radiating out from the leaf base, like the fingers of one's hand.

For those who appreciate color changes as the seasons move on, the leaves of Redbud have many surprises. The new leaves, appearing just after the flower buds have burst open, are a glossy coppery or bronzy color. Though they remain glossy, the color next changes to a bright green. Further maturation brings on a darker, blue-green color with a paler green underside. Before the leaves drop in fall, they turn a soft yellow. At its upper elevation limit, the leaves sometimes turn bright red in the fall.

Blossoming from February to April on last season's woody growth, Western Redbud is clothed with masses of magenta-colored flowers. Uncommonly, a plant may have white flowers. The umbel-like clusters, each with 2 to 5 flowers, are attached at the leaf nodes. The flower has 5 petals: the back, upright banner; two side wings; and two lower petals, the keel.

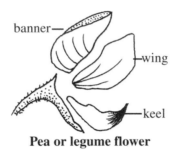

banner — wing — keel

Pea or legume flower

Look closely at a single flower. The deep magenta or wine-red sepals—the bud coverings—are fused at their bases. Unlike many flowers in the Pea or Legume Family, the light pink banner is the smallest of the 5 petals and is almost hidden on both sides by the delicate pinkish-white, 1/3-inch-long wing petals. The magenta-colored keel petals are cupped and face each other, opening only when an insect alights on them. When separated, the 1/2-inch-long keel petals reveal a white-tipped magenta-colored pistil and 10 greenish anthers. What a beauteous sight!

Maturing from May to August, each of the oblong-shaped, flat pods is 2 to 3 inches long and 1/2 inch wide. When first formed, the hanging pods are green, later turning to a wine-mauve and then to a reddish-brown that contrasts beautifully with the mature blue-green leaves. The pods are persistent and hang in clusters along the twigs for several months.

Eventually, the pod splits open—on one edge only—and the seeds are dispersed.

Redbud was seldom used as a source of food by the Native Californians, though a medicine made from the bark provided an astringent to treat diarrhea, dysentery and chills and fever.

The natives of northern California considered Redbud an important basketry plant, incorporating it both in twined and coiled baskets. Each fall, parts of the Redbud shrubs were pruned to encourage the growth of straight new shoots for harvesting the following spring.

The whole stems served as the red base for some coiled baskets; the split, peeled shoots provided long white wrapping strands. Slender twigs were sometimes separated into threads to use as sidewise strands or filler. Basket patterns were created with split, unpeeled red stems; either the red side or the white side could face outward. Redbud bark, steeped overnight in water and simmered the following day, provided a rose-tan dye.

One reference states that the genus name, *Cercis*, comes from the Greek word "kerkis" which was used as the genus name of a related plant which also has pod-like fruit—the Judas Tree. Another reference states that *Cercis* was derived from the Greek word "kerkis" meaning "a weaver's shuttle"—a reference to the similarity of the shape of the woody pods to that of the weaver's tool. The species name for Redbud, *occidentalis,* means "of the west" or "western".

Redbud is a shrub that is interesting year round: intricate branch patterns in the gray of winter, brilliant magenta floral displays in spring, changing leaf colors from spring to fall and dark, dangling reddish-brown pods from summer through winter. Take time to know this jewel throughout the year.

MANZANITAS

Among the numerous native shrubs blanketing the parched foothill chaparral, Manzanitas are probably more familiar to most people than any other genus. The genus, *Arctostaphylos*, is easily recognizable, but identification of the species can be most difficult, especially since several hybridize with other nearby species.

Mainly evergreen, they vary in height from a few inches to over 20 feet tall. The thick leathery leaves of the Manzanitas, arranged alternate on the stem, stand up edgewise, pointing their leaf tips toward the sky. This vertical alignment of the leaves minimizes exposure to the sun's rays, keeping the plant cooler and reducing the evaporation of moisture.

Immature, nascent flower buds develop in late summer and persist through winter until blossoming the following year. In late winter or early spring, you will discover these buds have turned into urn-shaped bells hanging in nodding clusters at the end of the stem. Manzanitas are members of the Heath Family and their bell-like flowers remind us of some other California relatives: huckleberries, white heather and madrone.

Immediately after blossoming, the plants send out new foliage and twig growth in tints of crimson or scarlet. Botanically-speaking, the fruits are small, berry-like drupes with 2 to 10 stones; they are not berries, nor are they pomes (little apples) as the common name suggests. Depending on the species, they vary in color from bright red to dull red to brownish red.

The bark is satiny smooth and richly colored. Varying with the species, it may be deep red, maroon, reddish purple, reddish brown or even chocolate brown in color. In late summer, the thin bark flakes off in small strips after the growing stems enlarge and split the skins open. The new bark is pale beige to light green in color and darkens with exposure to the sun.

In spring and summer, you might notice some reddish swellings on the edges of Manzanita leaves. These wounds, appearing only on new leaf growth, are caused by gall-forming insects—aphids, in the case of Manzanitas. (Each species of these insects produces an individual gall that is always the same size and shape and is specific to a plant genus.) The female aphids release chemical irritants as they feed on the succulent inner tissue. This causes the leaf to swell and eventually to fold over them. When you find a new red gall, open up the fold to discover the live aphids inside. Fortunately, the damage from these galls is minimal for the individual plants and large areas of chaparral usually do not become infested.

In northern California, Manzanita berries ranked second only to acorns in importance as a food source for Native Californians. Several tribes celebrated the ripening of the Manzanita berries with a harvest feast and dances.

The ripe berries, mealy and full of seeds, were eaten raw at the time of harvest or dried for later use. The pulverized berry pulp, with added water, made a tasty drink. The seeds were ground into flour, and after adding water, were either shaped into cakes and baked, or boiled to make a soup or mush.

Medicinally, a decoction of Manzanita leaves was taken as a diuretic. The juice from the leaves of some species of *Arctostaphylos* was used to treat skin sores and ulcers. A lotion made from the tannin-rich leaves relieved the dermatitis caused by Poison Oak.

Native Californians fashioned utensils such as spoons, scrapers and bowls from the dense, hard wood. They gathered long slender stems to make digging sticks and used forked branches as wood carriers.

Some have claimed that nails made from Manzanita wood were used in the building of Mission Dolores in San Francisco.

The common name, Manzanita, is from the Spanish word, "manzana" meaning "apple"; "manzanita" is the diminutive, meaning "little apple". The genus name, *Arctostaphylos*, originates from two Greek words: "arktos" meaning "bear" and "staphyle" meaning "bunch of grapes". Bears and coyotes, as well as other mammals and birds, are fond of these fruits.

COMMON MANZANITA

Common Manzanita, *Arctostaphylos manzanita*, is found in the foothills of the middle Inner Coast Ranges from Mount Diablo (in Contra Costa County), north to Shasta County, then south in the Sierra Nevada foothills to Mariposa County. It is most abundant in the lower foothill and valley flats of the gray pine belt; in some places, it extends up into the ponderosa pine forest at elevations below 5,000 feet. It is commonly seen on gravelly slopes of chaparral, woodlands and coniferous forests.

Common Manzanita is an erect, evergreen shrub with dark reddish-brown bark. It may range from 6 to 26 feet high, but is more commonly seen about 15 feet high. The many long, crooked branches are smooth, but the twigs are often covered with small, fine white hairs.

The thick, elliptic to oblong leaves are a bright shiny green on both sides. The leaves are 3/4 to 2 inches long and 1/2 to 1 1/2 inches wide. The leaf base is round to wedge-shaped. The margins (or edges) of the leaves are smooth, ending in an acute point at the leaf tip. The leaves are covered with minute hairs when young, but with age, the hairs are shed.

Four or five white petal lobes, 1/4 to 1/3 inch long, unite at their base to form an urn-shaped flower. Hanging upside-down, the flowers are bountiful from February to April. When the older flowers fall, the soil beneath the plant looks as if it is covered with a delicate silky-white sheet.

The fruits are round, smooth and about 1/2 inch in diameter. In early summer the berries are white, but change to a reddish-brown in late summer or fall. The Native Californians considered the berries of Common Manzanita to be of the poorest quality of all of the Manzanitas.

Common Manzanita does not stump- or crown-sprout after being cut or after fires, because it has no burl. (A burl, a large growth at a plant's base, connects the outer stems with the inner roots. From the burl, new shoots will sprout after severe pruning or fire damage.)

The meanings of the genus, species and common names are given in the preceding article titled "Manzanitas".

25

WHITELEAF MANZANITA

Whiteleaf Manzanita, *Arctostaphylos viscida*, is found on rocky slopes, in woodlands and chaparral, or in coniferous forests up to 6,000 feet in elevation; its upper range is about 1,000 feet above that of Common Manzanita.

Whiteleaf Manzanita grows from 3 to 12 feet tall. The smooth, deep red or reddish-brown bark covers the erect, compact branches of Whiteleaf Manzanita, though the hairiness of the twigs will vary from one subspecies to another.

The pale grayish-green or white leaves reflect more of the sunlight than do the darker green leaves of some manzanitas. This lighter color helps to keep the shrubs cooler in the hot foothills country. The leaves are 3/4 to 2 inches long and 3/4 to 1 1/2 inches wide. With short stems and rounded bases, they may be oval- or round-shaped. The margins are smooth or finely-toothed, ending in a sharp point at the tip.

Arranged in a many-flowered, compact panicle, the flowers bloom from February to April. The usually pink, but sometimes pinkish-white, bells contrast sharply with the light-colored leaves and give a soft touch to the spring scene. The reddish-brown berries are about 1/2 inch in diameter.

There are three subspecies of *Arctostaphylos viscida* recognized at this time: ssp. *mariposa*, ssp. *viscida* and ssp. *pulchella*. There are three differentiating factors: the area where the plant grows naturally, the hairiness (or lack of same) and the stickiness of the inflorescence, bracts or fruits. (A bract is a leaf-like structure either at the base of a solitary flower or under an entire cluster of flowers.)

Every part of Mariposa Manzanita, *Arctostaphylos viscida* ssp. *mariposa*, is covered with bristly hairs. Similar to fine sandpaper, the leaf is rough to the touch. Only the twigs and fruit are sticky. *A. v.* ssp. *mariposa* plants grow on rocky slopes, in woodlands, in chaparral or in coniferous forests of the Sierra Nevada—in a narrow belt of the mid-foothills from Amador County to Kern County, ranging from 2,000 to 6,000 feet elevation.

In contrast, *Arctostaphylos viscida* ssp. *viscida* is glabrous—without hairs. Only the bracts and stems of the inflorescence are sticky. (The inflorescence is the entire cluster of flowers on the main flower stem.) From 500 to 5,000 feet elevation, plants of ssp. *viscida* are found in chaparral and in coniferous forests of the Klamath Range, in the foothills of the Cascade Range of northern California and in the Sierra Nevada.

Arctostaphylos viscida ssp. *pulchella*, shares some of the characteristics of each of the other subspecies. While the twigs and leaves are glabrous, the bracts, flowers and fruit have fine bristly hairs. In addition, the bracts and fruit are sticky. Generally limited to the chaparral of the Klamath and North Coast Ranges, it is found from 600 to 3,000 feet elevation.

If you were in the Sierra Nevada, you would only have to compare the description of ssp. *mariposa* with that of ssp. *viscida* to identify the plant. Similarly, in the northwest mountain ranges, you need only consider ssp. *pulchella* and ssp. *viscida* for purposes of identification.

The species and subspecies name "*viscida*" means "sticky"; the subspecies name "*pulchella*" means "beautiful and little", while the subspecies name "*mariposa*" refers geographically to Mariposa County, California.

With the full moon reflecting off their white leaves, these are the manzanitas that light up the evening. In the daytime, flaunting their handsome pink bells, these are the ones that remain beautiful and attractive despite the hot, dry climate.

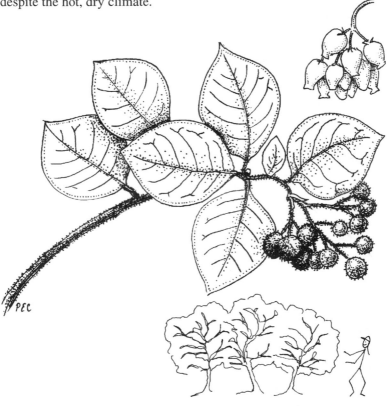

27

BEARBERRY

In California, Bearberry (*Arctostaphylos uva-ursi*) is found from sea level to 300 feet elevation in sandy soils, on coastal bluffs and on rocky outcroppings from the San Francisco Bay area north along the coast to the Oregon border. It also thrives high on the eastern slope of the central high Sierra Nevada, at elevations between 7,200 to 9,600 feet. Outside of California, Bearberry ranges from Oregon northward to Alaska; it is circumpolar in the northern hemispheres of North America, Europe and Asia. In Oregon, Native American tribes known to Lewis and Clark called this plant Kinnikinnick.

A mat-like shrub, rarely mounding, Bearberry usually is no more than 18 inches tall. The spreading branches or stems root readily where they contact the soil. The bark, reddish-brown in color, is sometimes rough to the touch. The twigs may be finely hairy or smooth. This species, *uva-ursi*, does not have burls and therefore will not stump-sprout after fires or cutting.

The leathery, oblong to oval leaves, 1/2 to 1 inch long and 1/4 to 1/2 inch wide, are rounded at the tips. They stand up edgewise, pointing the leaf tips skyward. The leaf margins are entire and rolled under or cupped. The upper surface of the leaves is shiny and dark green, while the underside is a lighter, pale green. The leaves turn a bronze color in the winter.

From March to May, the 1/4-inch-long flowers, white or pinkish-white, are arranged in short, few-flowered clusters at the end of the twigs. The globose fruits are bright red, 1/4 to 1/2 inch in diameter and glabrous. Birds and many mammals relish the berries; sometimes deer or other large animals will browse the leaves and small twigs.

A handsome shrub, Bearberry has been used extensively in public and home landscaping, especially in areas that are in close proximity to the California coast. It is used as an evergreen ground cover and provides excellent erosion control on bare slopes.

The genus name, *Arctostaphylos*, is from two Greek words: "arktos" meaning "bear" and "staphyle" meaning "bunch of grapes". The first part of the species name, *uva*, comes from the Latin word "uvarius" meaning "like a bunch of grapes"; the second part, *ursi,* refers to "ursus" or "bear". So, the names together mean "bear-bunch of grapes-bunch of grapes-bear!

One explanation of the origin of the common name, Bearberry, comes from an old folktale which described hungry bears that would search for the red berries of *A. uva-ursi* immediately upon waking from their winter sleep. (Bears and Bearberry plants often share habitat worldwide in the northern hemisphere.)

So, in three ways—from the common name, the genus name and the species name—it seems clear that bears have long been associated with the berries of this species. Was the person who gave this plant its genus and species names just playing with words, or testing our knowledge of Greek and Latin? Do you know of any other plant for which the meanings of the genus, the species and the common names are so nearly alike?

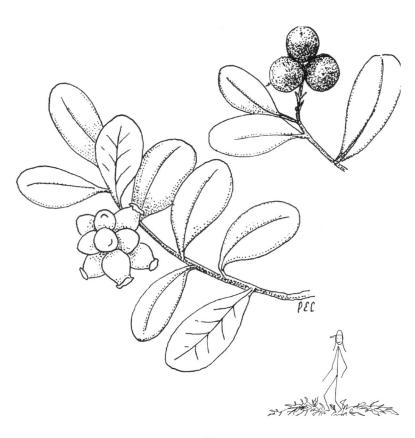

GREENLEAF MANZANITA

At elevations ranging from 2,500 to 11,000 feet, Greenleaf Manzanita, *(Arctostaphylos patula)* grows in open areas of mountain forests, woodlands and chaparral.

It ranges from the high mountains of the Outer North Coast Range to the Cascade Range, then south in the high Sierra Nevada to the San Gabriel, San Bernardino and San Jacinto Mountains of southern California. It is also found outside California: north to Oregon and Washington, east to Montana and Colorado and south to Baja California.

An erect or spreading shrub, it varies from 3 to 7 feet tall. Its bark is smooth and reddish-brown. Often many of the lower branches will root where the tips touch the ground. The species name, *patula*, is from the Latin meaning "spreading" or "open", relating to its open growth habit.

Only those shrubs of *A. patula* that grow in the central and southern High Sierra have burls and many trunks; the rest of the species' population in California have single trunks and lack burls. (Those Greenleaf Manzanita plants with burls may sprout after fires or severe cutting.)

Pointing skyward, the erect leaves are 1 to 2 1/2 inches long and 1/2 to 1 1/2 inches wide. They are ovate to round in shape, with a rounded or somewhat heart-shaped base. The leaf margins are entire—not notched, serrated or scalloped—and both leaf surfaces are similar: bright green, shiny and glabrous.

In May and June, the pink 1/4-inch-long flowers bloom in clusters on short stems. The flower stems, branches and bracts are covered with fine hairs and are sticky to the touch. The fruit, about 1/3 inch in diameter, is smooth and dark chestnut-brown. The Native Californians did not use these berries for food, although they ate berries of other manzanitas.

While deer and many large animals may browse this plant, bears, birds and small mammals eat only the berries.

Greenleaf Manzanita is abundant in mountainous forests and is readily identified by its spreading growth habit, bright green leaves, clusters of pink flowers and dark brown fruits. It sometimes hybridizes with other nearby Manzanita species, forming plants with intermediate characteristics of habit and leaf. Greenleaf Manzanita tolerates hot summers, cold winters and partial shade.

RHAMNUS and CEANOTHUS

The genera *Rhamnus* and *Ceanothus* are both members of the Buckthorn Family, and both are commonly seen in the chaparral of California. Some species of both genera may grow side by side in the wild.

In bloom, the tiny flowers of *Rhamnus* species are barely noticeable by sight, but their sweet scent announces their presence. Petals, if present, are white or green; the sepals and pedicels are gray or green. The flowers of the Redberrys have 4 sepals and no petals, while Coffeeberry flowers have 5 petals and usually 5 sepals. Arranged alternate on the stems, the leaves are pinnately-veined from the midrib. The veins are more prominent or visible on the undersides of the leaves. Also, the leaf veins of the Coffeeberrys are much more pronounced than those of the Redberrys. The fruit is a drupe with 2 or 3 separate stones. There are nine species of *Rhamnus* native to California.

In contrast, the fragrant flowers of *Ceanothus* ssp. are very showy: the sepals, petals and petal stems (pedicels) are all the same color, either white, blue or pink. Each flower has 5 sepals, 5 petals and 5 stamens. The leaves, one- to three-veined from their bases, are arranged alternate or opposite on the stems. The fruit is a three-seeded, round capsule, with or without horn-like projections. Over forty species of *Ceanothus* are native to California.

Caution: All parts of *Rhamnus* species (leaves, roots, bark and berries) should be considered *poisonous*. This is due to the severe purgative effect resulting from chewing or swallowing the bark, roots, leaves or berries.

HOLLY-LEAF REDBERRY

Formerly one *Rhamnus* species, Redberry has been separated into two species in *The Jepson Manual: Rhamnus ilicifolia* and *Rhamnus crocea*. Compared with *R. crocea, R. ilicifolia* has larger leaves and thornless branches.

In addition, Holly-leaf Redberry *(R. ilicifolia)* is more widely distributed and grows at a higher elevation than Spiny Redberry *(R. crocea)*. With the exception of the Sonoran Desert, the Modoc Plateau in northeastern California and the Great Basin, Holly-leaf Redberry is found throughout California.

Growing up to 6,000 feet in elevation, Holly-leaf Redberry prefers chaparral and mountainous forests. Highly variable, and even sometimes prostrate, this stout shrub often grows to 12 feet in height. Holly-leaf Redberry has stiff ascending branches and numerous short twigs.

The oval to almost round leaves, 1/2 to 1 1/4 inches across, are arranged alternate on the stem. The tips and bases of the evergreen leaves are round. Generally, the margins of the leaves have spiny or prickly, holly-like teeth. The undersides of the thick, bright green leaves are paler and often brownish in color. Depending on the habitat, the leaves may be glossy or dull. The leaf veins are not prominent, unlike some other *Rhamnus* species.

Blooming from February to April, the small clusters of 6 or fewer flowers are borne in the leaf axils. The tiny, yellowish-green, star-like flowers have 4 sepals, but no petals. Their fragrance attracts insects to the abundant nectar. The fruit is a drupe, oval in shape and about 1/4 inch wide. It is bright red and has 2 stones.

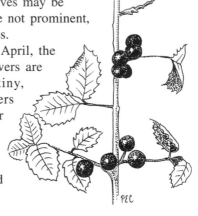

PEC

Holly-leaf Redberry was an important medicinal plant for the Native Californians. Preparations from the root or bark were used to treat many ills, including colds, sores and stomach ailments. Some other solutions were given as a laxative or diuretic. From the mashed ripe berries, they made poultices for use on sores.

The species name, *Rhamnus*, in ancient Greek, refers to Buckthorn, the common family name. *Ilicifolia* means "with holly-like leaves".

Caution: All parts of the *Rhamnus* species (leaves, roots, bark and berries) should be considered poisonous if ingested. This is due to the severe purgative effect resulting from chewing or swallowing any part of the *Rhamnus* plant.

SPINY REDBERRY

Once considered one species, Redberry has been separated into two species in *The Jepson Manual: Rhamnus crocea* and *Rhamnus ilicifolia.* Compared with Holly-leaf Redberry *(R. ilicifolia)*, Spiny Redberry *(R. crocea)* has smaller leaves and thorny branches.

While more frequently found in chaparral than Holly-leaf Redberry, Spiny Redberry also grows in coastal-sage scrub and woodlands from Napa County south to San Diego at elevations up to 3,000 feet. A low, densely-spreading shrub, Spiny Redberry usually grows up to 3 feet tall and about as wide. While the older branches are gray, the bark on the newer twigs is red to red-purple. The stout twigs are stiff, spreading and often thorn-tipped.

Arranged alternate on the stem, the leaves, almost round and 1/4 to 1/2 inch across, are pale to dark green above and brown or yellowish beneath. (This color may be responsible for the species name, *"crocea"* meaning "yellow".) The leaf veins of Spiny Redberry are not as prominent as those of other *Rhamnus* species. The leaf

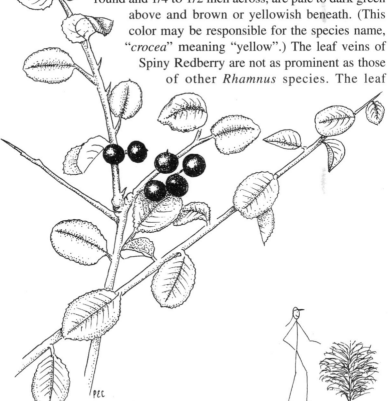

35

surfaces are smooth and the margins may be sharply toothed. Depending on habitat, the leaves may be glossy or dull.

From February to May, small clusters of 6 or less greenish-white flowers appear in the leaf axils. The flowers are tiny and have no petals. Each flower has 4 sepals and produces large quantities of nectar.

From July to September, the bright red, translucent fruits appear. Cylindrical in shape, each fruit has 2 stones and is about 1/4 inch long.

Native Californian medicinal uses of this plant can be found under Holly-leaf Redberry.

Spiny Redberry was introduced into England in 1848 by plant collector Theodor Hartweg (1812-1871). The genus name, *Rhamnus*, in ancient Greek, was the name for the Buckthorn—the common family name. (The species name, *crocea*, was discussed earlier in this article.)

Caution: All parts of the *Rhamnus* species (leaves, roots, bark and berries) should be considered poisonous if chewed or swallowed. This is due to the severe purgative effect resulting from ingestion of any part of the *Rhamnus* plant.

CALIFORNIA COFFEEBERRY

One of the most common shrubs of the California Coast Range, California Coffeeberry *(Rhamnus californica)* is widely distributed in the West—from Washington State south to Baja California, then east to the Rockies. In California, it grows along the entire coast and in the coastal mountains below 7,500 feet elevation. California Coffeeberry prefers the full sun of dry hillsides, and is found in chaparral, oak woodlands or mixed evergreen forests.

An open-branched shrub that may reach 15 feet in height, it usually is about 6 or 7 feet tall and 4 to 5 feet wide. In contrast with the rigid stems of the Redberrys, the stems of Coffeeberry are flexible. The bark is bright gray or brown and the surface of the twigs is more commonly smooth, yet at times it may be finely hairy.

The evergreen leaves are dark green above and paler beneath. They are arranged alternate on the stem; usually both leaf surfaces are smooth. The oval to elliptic leaves are 1 to 3 inches long and 1/2 to 1 inch wide.

The prominent pinnate veins curve upward in a parallel pattern from the midrib to the leaf margin. These lateral veins are more noticeable on the paler undersides of the leaves.

The leaves of California Coffeeberry are most variable: the margins may be serrate or smooth and sometimes rolled under; the leaf base and the leaf tip may be acute or rounded. Additionally, the size and texture of the leaves seems to be related to their habitat: small and thick in drier habitats, large and thin in moister, shady situations.

Up to 60 greenish-white, star-like flowers, mostly inconspicuous, are borne in an umbel at the end of an inch-long stem. Each tiny flower, blooming from April to June, has 5 petals and yields copious amounts of nectar that surely delight the insects.

In July and August, the Coffeeberry fruit ripens. After changing color from green to red, then to a shiny black, the mature 1/3- to 1/2-inch drupe consists of a thin watery pulp surrounding 2 or 3 stony pits.

The Native Californians knew of Coffeeberry's medicinal virtues long before the Spanish Californians arrived. The natives stripped the bark from the plant in spring or autumn and dried it; then it was aged for at least a year. Later, they used it to steep a brew to treat rheumatism or to provide a laxative effect.

To early European settlers, *Rhamnus californica* seeds resembled the berries of *Coffea arabica*—the commercially-grown coffee plant— in shape and appearance. They hoped they had found a coffee substitute. However, its bitter flavor kept it from being a successful substitute. Nevertheless, the common name persists.

Some other common names include Yellow Bay, Yellow Root and Bitter Bark.

The word *Rhamnus* is derived from an ancient Greek name for Buckthorn, the common family name. The species name, *californica*, means "of California". The Spanish padres called this plant "cascara sagrada" meaning "sacred bark". Many birds and mammals relish the berries and leaves of Coffeeberry.

Caution: All parts of *Rhamnus* species (leaves, roots, bark and berries) should be considered toxic if ingested. This is due to the severe purgative effect resulting from chewing or swallowing of any part of the *Rhamnus* plant.

CLEMATIS

The native *Clematis* is a woody deciduous vine. In the wild, it grows on or over shrubs and small trees, often making a leafy shelter or bower. Two species of *Clematis* are widely distributed in California: Virgin's Bower, *C. ligusticifolia*, and Pipestems, *C. lasiantha*.

Clematis, unlike many vines, does not have tendrils that twine around vegetation or other support, but rather climbs by means of its leaf stalks or petioles. The petioles bend, clasp or wrap around any nearby plants.

Darwin, the naturalist, was interested in the leaf movements of *Clematis*. He observed that the plant was sensitive to touch and that the leaves would fold over if rubbed on the underside. If there was nothing to cling to, they would straighten out again in a few hours. Additionally, he found that the young shoots of the leaf stalk followed the path of the sun throughout the day.

Clematis has thin, light green leaves arranged opposite on the stems. The pinnately compound leaflets may be lobed or toothed.

Though *Clematis* blossoms have no petals, the fragrant flowers are showy due to their hairy, white- to cream-colored sepals. (The sepals of most flowers are greenish in color.) Additionally, *Clematis* flowers have numerous pistils and stamens. The flower stems are found in the leaf axil, the upper angle where the leaf attaches to the stem.

The flowers of some *Clematis* species are dioecious, having their stamens and pistils on separate plants. From a distance, the flowers with the stamens are more showy than those with the greenish-white pistils, because the stamens' bright yellow color stands out boldly.

Clematis has a persistent style that connects the stigma with its seed-producing base—the ovary. (For more information, see the illustrations in the front of the book.) The fruit is a cluster or head of one-seeded achenes, each with an elongated style that develops into a plumose tail. These tails aid in the wind dispersal of the seeds.

Though they did not use *Clematis* as a food plant, Native Californians found many other uses for *Clematis*. They boiled the stems and bark of *Clematis* in water for use as an inhalant to treat colds. Charcoal made from the stems was pulverized, then dusted on burns and sores. The leaves, bark or roots were dried, then ground into a powder for use as a soap or shampoo.

Caution: The leaves of all *Clematis* should be considered poisonous.

VIRGIN'S BOWER

Virgin's Bower, *C. ligusticifolia*, flourishes below 8,000 feet elevation, preferring wet places, either along streams or in canyon bottoms. When its moisture needs are met, it can be found all over California, then up to British Columbia, east to South Dakota and south down to New Mexico and northwest Mexico. A vigorous climber, Virgin's Bower stretches up to a height of 40 feet, while some of its side branches reach 15 feet in length. The older stems have gray shreddy bark.

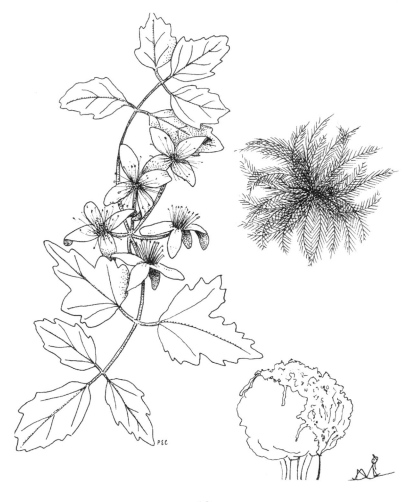

Virgin's Bower usually has 5 to 7 smooth leaflets and their leaf margins are either lobed or toothed. The leaves are 3/4 to 3 inches long and have a peppery scent when crushed. (Another common name is Pepper Vine.)

Virgin's Bower blooms in March and April. The greenish-white flowers, each 1/2 to 3/4 inches across, have 4 sepals and are arranged in a many-flowered panicle. Despite their small size, the profusion of blossoms almost covers the entire plant when it is in bloom.

These blossoms form a white cloak over the supporting chaparral; from a distance, the plant has the wispy, silky appearance of a bridal veil. Probably, it is from its growth habit and its flowers that it derives one of its common names—Virgin's Bower.

The fruit of Virgin's Bower makes a most dramatic display. From the base of the seed cluster, the style of each seed grows into a feathery gray-white tail—1/2 to 1 inch long. Then all of the plumose tails from one flower are twisted into a shape resembling a silvery ball, 2 to 2 1/4 inches across. These balls reflect the sunlight when the angle is right, and the fuzzy tails are transformed into a mass of glistening silver.

Clematis is an ancient name for a climbing plant from the Greek word, "klema", meaning "twig". *Ligusticifolia* is said to be derived from Latin and means "leaves like those of the genus *Ligusticum*", although this author fails to see the resemblance.

Caution: The leaves of all *Clematis* should be considered poisonous.

PIPESTEMS

Pipestems, *C. lasiantha*, is found at elevations less than 7,000 feet. In contrast to Virgin's Bower, Pipestems prospers under more arid conditions, provided its "feet" are damp or in the shade. It is found in chaparral or woodlands of the coastal areas of central and southern California; in the South Coast, Transverse and Peninsular Ranges; and in the Sierra Nevada. Smaller than Virgin's Bower, Pipestems will grow to 20 to 30 feet, often reaching those heights in a single season. The fuzzy leaflets of *C. lasiantha* are in threes, coarsely toothed and 1 to 2 inches long.

Blooming in April and May, each flower of Pipestems is solitary, borne on a single stem up to 6 inches long. The flowers are large (1 to 2 inches wide) and have 4 sepals. There is such an abundance of stems and flowers that the vine seems to illuminate the hillside or canyon with a bright cream color. However, the display of the fruit of Pipestems is not as spectacular as that of Virgin's Bower.

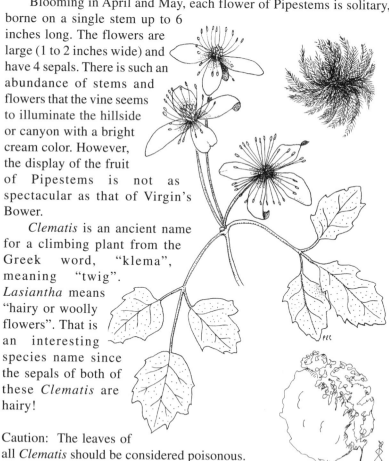

Clematis is an ancient name for a climbing plant from the Greek word, "klema", meaning "twig". *Lasiantha* means "hairy or woolly flowers". That is an interesting species name since the sepals of both of these *Clematis* are hairy!

Caution: The leaves of all *Clematis* should be considered poisonous.

A BIT ABOUT THE GENUS, PRUNUS

Generally, California native species of the genus *Prunus* branch in many directions forming impenetrable shrub masses. Botanically, the fruit of this genus is called a drupe. It has a fleshy or soft outside covering a stony pit; the pit, when cracked, yields a one-seeded kernel hidden inside.

Except for the Sierra Plum, Holly-leafed Cherry and Western Choke-Cherry, the flesh of *Prunus* species was not usually eaten by Native Californians as it was extremely bitter and pungent. However, several tribes harvested the kernels of the stones, which they further processed. Before using the shoots, leaves, bark or seeds for food or medicine, the Native Californians processed them by leaching, heating or boiling or a combination thereof.

Prunus shoots, peeled and split, were used in basketry by some tribes. Sometimes, the shoots were inserted as a decorative overlay in basket patterns. Various tools, such as digging sticks, arrows and arrow foreshafts were made from the wood.

Caution: The shoots, leaves, bark and seeds of most species of the genus *Prunus* are toxic to humans as they contain hydrocyanic acid.

SIERRA PLUM

Sierra Plum, *Prunus subcordata,* prospers in mixed evergreen or coniferous forests up to 6,300 feet in elevation. It grows along the North Coast and in the Klamath, North Coast and Cascade Ranges. It also thrives along the Central Coast and in the Central Coast Ranges (including the San Francisco Bay area) south to San Luis Obispo County. Sierra Plum is also found inland, though often sparsely, throughout the entire length of the Sierra Nevada and its foothills, and south to Kern County. (It is not found in the Great Central Valley.)

Though it can reach up to 25 feet, this erect, deciduous shrub is more often seen as a 6 to 12 foot shrub. The large, rough branches, gray-brown in color, are stiff and crooked; some of their short twigs end in sharp woody spines. Sierra Plum forms thickets as its underground stems, or rhizomes, often sprout and form new plants at its nodes.

The shiny gray bark is marked by bands of lenticels reminiscent of those of the cultivated cherry. These lenticels—openings on the bark of woody twigs—are breathing pores that permit exchange of oxygen and carbon dioxide between the atmosphere and the inner living tissue.

The dark green leaves, 1 to 2 inches long and 1/2 to 1 1/2 inches wide, are elliptical to ovate in shape. The leaf base may be rounded or barely heart-shaped. As in many *Prunus* species, the leaf margins are finely-serrate. The leaves turn a bright red before falling.

Blooming in March and April, the flowers occur singly or in clusters of 2 to 4. The white or pink blossoms appear soon after the leaf emerges in mid-spring. (Some observers say that the flowers are always white when opening, but turn pink as they age.) About 1/2 to 3/4 inch across, the fragrant flowers have 5 petals and many stamens.

Ripening in August and September, the fruits are oblong, 1/2 to 1 inch long and bright red or yellow; they contain a stony pit. Sierra Plum's flower color, fruit color and edibility vary widely throughout the state. For example, in its northern range, the fruit is larger and juicier than it is in southern California.

Prunus, the genus name, means "plum". The species, *subcordata,* refers to the shape of the leaf base. In Latin, the prefix "sub" means "not completely", while "cordatus" means "heart-shaped".

Sierra Plum was first collected by Theodor Hartweg (1812-1871), probably in 1846 or 1847, for the London Horticultural Society. It is the largest stone fruit native to the Sierra Nevada.

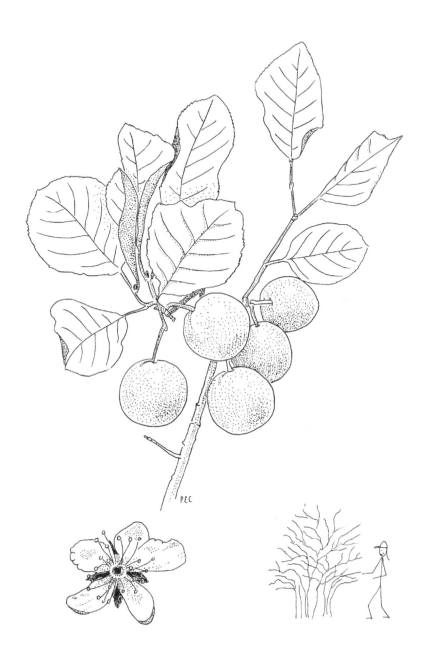

Caution: See "A Bit About the Genus, *Prunus*" for this information.

HOLLY-LEAFED CHERRY

Holly-leafed Cherry, *Prunus ilicifolia* ssp. *ilicifolia*, is found on slopes or in canyons of woodlands or shrublands up to 5,000 feet in elevation. It grows in the North Coast Ranges in Napa, Solano and Sonoma Counties, and in the Central Coast and Central Coast Ranges from the San Francisco Bay area south to Baja California.

This multi-stemmed evergreen shrub can reach 50 feet in height and be nearly as broad. However, under less favorable conditions, it may only reach 20 feet. In its native habitat, Holly-leafed Cherry does not grow very tall due to fires and animal browsing. Tolerant of desert and seacoast conditions, it also endures cold down to 10° F, but not for prolonged periods of time. It withstands drought, but prospers with summer watering—assuming excellent drainage has been provided.

The bark of the twigs is reddish-brown to gray. Though densely branched, Holly-leafed Cherry can be pruned to tree form. However, considerable maintenance is necessary to remove the suckers and unwanted branches to keep it in an arboreal or tree-like shape.

The margins of the holly-like, evergreen leaves are serrate with spiny teeth. The leathery leaves are 3/4 to 4 3/4 inches long and ovate to round in shape. When crushed, the crisp leaves emit a scent of almond. Deeply veined, the upper leaf surfaces are dark green and shiny; underneath, they are a dull yellowish-green.

From March to May, the creamy-white flowers, about 1/4 inch wide, appear with the newly emerging bright green leaves. The narrow, unbranched clusters of flowers, up to 2 inches long, hang loosely from the leaf axils; they are not as pendulous as are those of the Western Choke-Cherry. As with other *Prunus* species, the flowers have 5 petals and many stamens.

In late summer to early fall, the 1/2- to 3/4-inch fruits mature to a bright red. The one-seeded stony pit is covered with a thin layer of sweet fleshy pulp.

The Native Californians had several uses for Holly-leafed Cherry. It was an important food source for several tribes. They ate the fruit freshly picked from the shrub and also pressed the fruit to make a drink.

However, it was the seeds or kernels that made a larger contribution to the total food supply than did the fruit pulp. After drying, the pits were cracked open and the kernels were crushed in a mortar. The resultant meal was then leached by pouring several rinses of water over it. After boiling the mash to reduce or eliminate the toxic acids, it was eaten as a gruel or soup. A thicker mash was shaped into cakes.

Medicinally, the Native Californians boiled the leaves in water to use as a wash to treat headaches, and they made a tea from the bark as a remedy for colds.

The common name, Holly-leafed Cherry, and the species' and subspecies' names, "*ilicifolia*", are references to the holly-like leaves. Some other common names are Evergreen Cherry, Spanish Wild Cherry and Islay.

The fruit is eaten by birds and rodents and the foliage is heavily browsed by deer, elk and other mammals.

Caution: See "A Bit About the Genus, *Prunus*" for this information.

WESTERN CHOKE-CHERRY

On rocky slopes or in canyons, Western Choke-Cherry covers hundreds of acres of chaparral, mixed evergreen pine forests and other coniferous forests. With the exception of coastal areas, the Great Central Valley and the desert, it is found throughout California at elevations from nearly sea level to the high mountains below 9,500 feet. Outside of California, *Prunus virginiana* var. *demissa* grows north to British Columbia, east to the central United States, south to Texas and northern Mexico.

A graceful shrub, Western Choke-Cherry may reach up to 20 feet, but more often it is found from 12 to 15 feet. The branches of Western Choke-Cherry are flexible and the stems are grayish. Their tips are not thorn-like as are those of Sierra Plum. The young twigs may be covered with gray hairs that fall off with age. The bark varies in color from dark red to red-purple to brown. Lenticels are present on the older stems.

The deciduous leaves are large, measuring 2 1/2 to 3 1/2 inches long and 3/4 to 2 inches wide. They are arranged alternate on the stem, either singly or in clusters of 2 or 3. The round to elliptic leaves are finely serrate with sharply-pointed leaf tips. There are 2 glands on each petiole

just below its attachment to the leaf. The dark green leaves turn to a bright yellow before dropping in the fall.

Blooming in April and May, the five-petalled white flowers emit a pleasing fragrance. At the ends of the short leafy branches, numerous 1/2-inch flowers are crowded into dense cylindrical clusters, 2 to 4 inches long.

In August and September, the dark red to black cherries in many-fruited clusters hang down from the ends of the branches. The cherries are round and 1/4 to 1/2 inch in diameter. The pulp covering the pit is fleshy, bitter and astringent, especially if eaten before the fruit is fully ripe. (Medically, "astringent" means "causing constriction of soft tissue". The common name may have arisen from the biting taste, which might have caused someone to choke.)

The Native Californians made pemmican and a soup from the cherries. Medicinally, they used the inner bark of the shrub to brew a tea to treat diarrhea and colds and to use as a sedative or tonic. In addition, this tea was thought to improve hoarseness. The bark was also boiled in water to make a lotion to bathe wounds.

The genus name, *Prunus*, means "plum"; the species name, *virginiana*, "of Virginia". The variety *demissa*, is derived from a Latin word that means "drooping", undoubtedly referring both to the flower cluster and the fruit.

Wildlife eat the foliage; birds and bears relish the fruit.

Caution: The immature fruit and pits, as well as the young shoots, contain cyanogenic substances and should be avoided.

BITTER CHERRY

Found at elevations up to 9,200 feet in California, Bitter Cherry, *Prunus emarginata*, grows on rocky slopes and in canyons of chaparral, mixed evergreen or coniferous forests. Bitter Cherry grows throughout California except in the San Joaquin and Sacramento Valleys and in the Great Basin and Desert Provinces. It is found in habitats similar to that of Western Choke-Cherry. Outside of California, it is found in British Columbia, Idaho, Nevada and Arizona.

Usually a deciduous shrub about 4 to 12 feet high, Bitter Cherry is rarely arboreal or tree-like in the wild. Unlike those of Western Choke-Cherry, the branches are rigid and stiff. Bitter Cherry spreads by underground stems creating small colonies or thickets. The older stems and branches are usually silvery gray and marked with bands of lenticels—similar to those of ornamental or commercially-grown cherry trees. The bark on the young slender twigs is shiny-red, but ages to gray.

Arranged alternate on older branches, the deciduous leaves are generally attached on the stems in clusters of 2 to 5. Obovate in shape, the leaves are 3/4 to 2 inches long and 3/8 to 1 inch wide. They are finely toothed and fold inward; there is a pair of glands at the wedge-shaped leaf base. The leaves are dark green and hairless above, and green and hairy or hairless below. In fall, they turn a golden yellow before floating to the ground.

Soon after the shrub has leafed out, 3 to 12 flowers appear in short clusters—which are more or less flat-topped. Blooming from April to July, each of the 1/2-inch white blossoms has 5 petals, 5 sepals and a myriad of stamens. When in bloom, open thickets of Bitter Cherry emit an almond-like fragrance.

From late summer into fall, the oval- to round-shaped cherries ripen. The fruit, a drupe or stone fruit, is smooth and 1/3 to 1/2 inch long. Fleshy pulp surrounds the stone-like pit that contains the seed. The fruit changes in color from green to bright red, then to red-purple—the cherries are almost black at maturity.

The Native Californians used the leaves to make an aqueous extract to treat bruises, sprains and inflammation, as well as some facial rashes. The medication made from the leaves was also considered a tonic to be taken for many ills. In basketry, Bitter Cherry bark was sometimes blended into a design.

The genus name, *Prunus*, is the Latin name for the plum tree; *emarginata* means "with a shallow notch at the tip", perhaps referring

50

to the petal tip. The biting, pungent taste of the fruit undoubtedly accounts for two common names: Bitter Cherry and Quinine Cherry. The inedible Bitter Cherry is more commonly seen in its native environment than are the other indigenous stone fruits.

Caution: Though relished by birds, the bitter pulp is considered inedible for humans. There are some reports of Bitter Cherry causing illness.

SOURBERRY

One of the most widely distributed western shrubs, Sourberry, (*Rhus trilobata*) is found in washes or canyon bottoms of the lower foothills, on lightly-shaded slopes in the drier parts of the mountains or in the high mountains of the Mojave Desert. It grows up to 7,200 feet in elevation in every part of California except for the Modoc Plateau of northeastern California, the Great Basin and the Sonoran Desert. Outside of California, it extends from Alberta, Canada, south through the Rockies to Colorado and Texas, then over to Utah, New Mexico, Arizona and northern Mexico.

A graceful shrub with arching branches that droop at the tips, Sourberry can reach 8 feet in height. In sharp contrast with the stiff, upright growing habit of Poison Oak, Sourberry is a widely-branched, spreading shrub. However, both plants can form dense thickets. On hot summer days, the smooth brown bark of Sourberry gives off a strong medicinal odor when rubbed.

Additionally, the foliage, when crushed, is strongly scented. As Sourberry is a member of the Sumac Family, that odor may explain the origin of two common names: Scented Sumac and Fragrant Sumac. Some observers state that it has a potent and disagreeable odor; that observation may account for another common name, Skunkbrush.

A quick glance at this shrub might lead some to think it was Poison Oak because of the phrase "leaves of three, let it be". Sourberry does have leaves made up of 3 leaflets. They are usually pinnately compound, and the terminal leaflet is larger than the side ones and can be 2 inches long. However, unlike the shiny, bright green leaves of Poison Oak, the dull green leaves of Sourberry are slightly fuzzy. In addition, the terminal wedge-shaped leaflet of Sourberry is not petioled (meaning that it has no stem), while the terminal leaflet of Poison Oak has a distinct stem.

In March and April, the tiny bell-shaped flowers—in terminal spikes about 1/2 to 1 inch long—bloom before the leaves emerge. The petals are generally pale yellow, and the sepals, yellow-green to reddish in color.

Covered with sticky hairs, the one-seeded orange or red drupes are about 1/4 inch in diameter. A deciduous shrub, Sourberry makes a colorful display in the fall with its bright orange and red leaves.

Sourberry was an important plant to the Native Californians, providing food, medicine and basketry materials. The sticky berries were eaten fresh; or, they were dried, then ground and made into a soup. Sometimes, the berries were mashed, then soaked in water to make a pleasant-tasting acidic drink.

Medicinally, the ground berries were used for treatment of stomach ailments and a lotion was prepared from them to treat sores. An aqueous extract of the crushed stems provided relief from coughing and lung ailments.

In making coiled baskets, the Native Californians used the young and slender branches of the Sourberry plant; these were much tougher than those of willows. They soaked, scraped and then split the thin, flexible stems or twigs into several strands to wrap around a basket's Deergrass base. The undyed cordage, naturally a light straw color, was sometimes darkened by soaking it in an elderberry dye for two or more weeks.

For making twined baskets, Sourberry was one of the most valuable sources of basket materials in central and southern California as well as in Utah, Arizona and New Mexico. (Two other California species of the genus *Rhus*, *integrifolia* and *ovata*, were not used in basketmaking.)

Rhus is from "rhous"—the old Greek name used to designate the genus containing the Sumacs; *trilobata* means "three-lobed". The common name Sourberry, probably was chosen because of the tart taste of the berries. (The origins of three other common names were mentioned earlier.)

Though Sourberry is in the same family as Poison Oak, its leaves, stems and fruit do not produce the distressing dermatitis associated with Poison Oak.

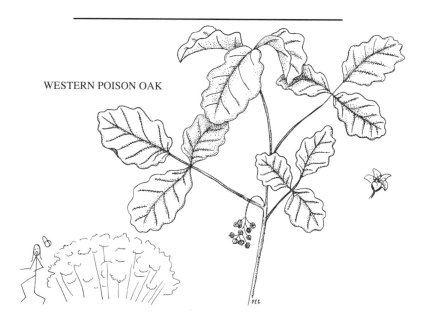

WESTERN POISON OAK

54

WESTERN POISON OAK

Western Poison Oak, *Toxicodendron diversilobum*, probably is more widespread than any other native plant. It ranges over a wide area in California—similar to the distribution of Sourberry, *Rhus trilobata*. Both are members of the Sumac Family, and *T. diversilobum* generally favors the habitat of Sourberry, but it prefers lower elevations than Sourberry. Only growing up to 5,500 feet in elevation, it is found in canyons or on slopes of chaparral and oak woodlands from British Columbia to Baja California. It is rarely found in redwood forests.

The growth habit of Poison Oak is extremely variable. It can grow as a low ground cover to 2 feet high, form dense thickets as a stiff, upright shrub 6 to 13 feet high or climb the trunks of large forest trees to 80 feet.

The stems are gray to red-brown with black mottling; they may be either smooth or hairy. The leaves are 3 to 6 inches long, and the leaf stem—the petiole—is up to 4 inches long. The pinnately compound leaves are divided into 3, sometimes 5, leaflets that are shiny, egg-shaped, hairless and 2 1/2 to 5 inches long. The margins are entire, wavy or slightly lobed. The terminal leaflet, up to 5 inches long and 3 inches wide, has a long stalk and is much larger than the side leaflets; the lateral leaflets are nearly sessile—without stems.

When the leaves first appear in spring, they are a bronzy red, later becoming a shiny bright green. They change to a brilliant red in autumn— one of the few sources of red in the fall color mosaic of California.

Appearing as the leaves emerge in April and May, the drooping clusters of yellow-green, 1/8-inch-wide flowers branch out from the leaf axil. The highly fragrant flowers invite the bees to partake of their nectar. The round, berry-like drupes, about 1/4 inch in diameter, are creamy-white and marked with black ridges; they have a hard stone inside.

Native Californians made some use of the leaves, sap and stems of Poison Oak. However, they also reported using plants, among them *Grindelia* species (Gumweed), *Artemesia* species (Mugwort), Toyon, Manzanita, Milkweed species, California Coffeeberry, Yerba Santa and Soap Plant, to relieve the rash and sores caused by Poison Oak. It would seem that many native people did not have immunity from the poisonous effects of Poison Oak.

Urushiol, the chemical responsible for the rash caused by Poison Oak, is a thick, clear, non-volatile oil. Within minutes of contact, the oil is absorbed into the skin. A quick washing with soap (or rubbing the skin with soil or water if in the wild) may decrease the severity of the dermatitis.

This oil will remain on clothing, including shoes, and also on a pet's fur, until carefully cleaned off. Hopping into a sleeping bag with Poison Oak-contaminated clothes may cause dermatitis each time the bag is used, unless it is cleaned before it is used again.

Rather than eradicating Poison Oak and upsetting the food balance of nature, perhaps humans should stand back and enjoy the beauty of Poison Oak from a distance, while allowing our fellow animal inhabitants of this planet to enjoy the shrubs for their food. Deer, elk and small mammals browse the leaves and stems. The berries are an important food source for game birds such as quail, grouse and wild turkey, as well as many other birds, including songbirds. Many other animals also relish the berries.

Several features distinguish toxic Poison Oak from the innocuous "look-alike" Sourberry: the branches of Poison Oak are stiff and upright while those of Sourberry arch; the leaves of Poison Oak are green and shiny, while those of Sourberry are dull green and fuzzy; the leaflets of Poison Oak are almost twice the size of Sourberry leaflets; the stalk of the terminal leaflet of Poison Oak is up to 4 inches long, but the terminal leaflet of Sourberry has no stalk at all; the flowers of Poison Oak are in loose drooping clusters, while those of Sourberry are in a tight upright raceme; and Poison Oak berries are creamy-white with dark ridges, while the berries of Sourberry are orange-red.

Toxicodendron means "poisonous tree"; *diversilobum* means "diversely or variously lobed", which refers to the margins of the leaf. Poison Oak is another California native that sprouts vigorously after fires or severe pruning.

Caution: Year round, any part of this native plant may cause severe dermatitis in susceptible persons. The degree of toxicity to individual persons is not known until after exposure. For some, this may be too late to prevent severe reactions. So, avoid contact with Poison Oak under all circumstances.

OREGON-GRAPE

Native to the Sierra Nevada, Cascade, North Coast and Klamath Ranges, Oregon-Grape (*Berberis aquifolium* var. *aquifolium*) grows in coniferous forests from 1,300 to 7,000 feet in elevation. It is not found in the California deserts. Outside California, its range extends north to Canada.

The ascending to erect, freely-branching stems of this evergreen shrub generally arise from rhizomes (underground stems); these rhizomes produce roots from their lower surfaces and send up shoots from their upper surfaces. These roots, tough and hard, are a bright golden yellow. Oregon-Grape is usually less than 7 feet high; its branches are purplish-brown and the inner bark and wood are a bright yellow.

Oregon-Grape leaves are arranged alternate on the stem and vary from 4 to 10 inches in length. Though the new leaf growth is bronzy in color, the glossy odd-pinnately compound leaves mature to a bright green. The 5 to 9 leaflets, each 1 to 3 inches long and 3/4 to 1 3/4 inches wide, are ovate to elliptical in shape. Holly-like and prickly to the touch, each leaflet has 12 to 24 spiny teeth on its wavy edges. A few of the leaves turn bright red in the fall before falling to the ground.

From March to May, dense clusters of bright yellow flowers appear

57

at the top of the stem. Each of the 30 to 60 tiny flowers in the rounded 1 1/4- to 2 1/2-inch-wide cluster has 6 petals. Pollinated by native solitary bees, the flowers have a clean, sweet fragrance welcomed by all, but especially by bees and those humans who have a low tolerance for perfume.

From May to July, the 1/4-inch egg-shaped fruit ripens. The berries are dark blue, covered with a whitish, waxy film or bloom, giving them a bluish-gray color.

To horticulturalists, Oregon-Grape is known under two generic names: *Mahonia* and *Berberis*. Some botanists place all compound-leaved barberries, including Oregon-Grape, in the genus *Mahonia*, while others retain the Oregon-Grape with the simple-leaved barberries in the genus *Berberis*. *The Jepson Manual* places Oregon-Grape in the genus *Berberis*.

Oregon-Grape was an important plant to the Native Californians. The berries were eaten either raw or cooked, and some of the berries were dried and stored for later use. Ground dried berries were mixed with dried salmon to make pemmican.

The Native Californians used great care in preparing medicines from Oregon-Grape as some parts of this plant (especially the roots) were considered toxic. The Native Californians made medicinal teas from the leaves or root bark to stimulate the appetite, or to treat coughs, stomach problems and kidney ailments. In addition, an aqueous solution prepared from the roots was used as an eye wash or as a lotion to reduce inflammation. Beargrass, an important basketry material, was dyed a brilliant yellow using the roots and bark of Oregon-Grape.

Oregon-Grape was first grown in the eastern United States from seed collected by members of the 1804-1806 Lewis and Clark Expedition. (They called this plant Shiny Oregon Grape.) In 1823, famous plant explorer David Douglas (1799-1834) obtained *Berberis aquifolium* plants from an eastern nursery and introduced the species to England.

Berberis is Latin for the ancient Arabic name for Barberry. Also Latin, "aqui" means "sharp", and *aquifolium* means "sharp-leaved", a reference to the sharp spines on the edges of the leaflets.

Caution: Most parts of this plant, especially the roots, are considered toxic.

SOMETHING ABOUT CEANOTHUS

According to *The Jepson Manual*, there are 45 species of *Ceanothus*, or California-Lilac, in North America. Another common name for this genus is Red Root, as the roots yield a red dye upon processing. They are found especially in the West, and 43 of the species are native to California. The plants in this genus fall into two distinct groups based on leaf, flower or fruit characteristics.

One group of plants has leaves that are arranged alternate on the stems; the leaves are generally thin and can be evergreen or deciduous. The flowers appear in dense racemes or panicles. The fruit, a three-celled capsule, is without horns, but may have crests or ridges.

The other group of plants has leaves arranged opposite on the stems, with thick, often flat, evergreen leaves. The flowers are in racemes only, and the three-celled capsule generally has horns, with or without crests or ridges.

In both groups, the branches are frequently arranged on the trunks in the same manner as the leaves on the stems. For example, if the leaves are arranged alternate on the stems, the branches are most often arranged alternate on the trunks.

BUCK BRUSH

The most common and widespread species of the genus *Ceanothus* in California, *C. cuneatus* var. *cuneatus* is found on dry rocky slopes or ridges, or in sandy or rocky soils below 6,000 feet elevation. Up to 10 feet tall, Buck Brush, a rigid, upright, evergreen plant, grows throughout the state except in the Great Central Valley. Buck Brush is also found in Oregon and northern Baja California. A prominent component of the chaparral, the branches of Buck Brush are so twiggy and interlaced that they create a nearly impenetrable thicket. Arranged opposite on the trunk, the light gray, smooth branches darken with age.

The dull green leaves, arranged opposite on the spur-like twigs, do not have petioles (leaf stems). Unlike the smooth upper surface of the leaf, the underside is covered with fine, dense grayish-white hairs. One prominent vein arises from the leaf base.

Vertically-oriented, the 1 1/4-inch-long wedge-shaped leaves absorb less heat than if their leaf surfaces were in a flat plane; this helps keep the plant cooler. In addition, the light gray color of the twigs and bark reflects some of the sun's rays causing less dehydration in the hot dry environment.

Scattered among the leaves, the umbel-like clusters of tiny flowers are about an inch long. When in bloom from March to May, the white blossoms so thoroughly cover the plants, and the plants are so abundant, that the slopes appear to be covered with a light snow. The flowers are rarely blue or lavender in color. They give off a spicy scent, enjoyed by some, yet despised by others. Each globose fruit, less than 1/4 inch in diameter, generally has 3 short horns near the top of its three-celled capsule. The seeds germinate rapidly after fires and huge colonies can be formed in a few short years.

Native Californians used Buck Brush seed for food. They brewed a tea from the leaves and flowers to treat coughs, fevers and colds. Infusions made from the bark served as an astringent or tonic.

The sticky fruits, when dampened with water, made a soapy lather. The blossoms, also producing suds in water, were used for washing hair or as a wash for the skin, eliciting one of the plant's common names, Soap Bush.

Ceanothus comes from a Greek word meaning "spiny plant"; *cuneatus* means "wedge-shaped", referring to the leaf shape—broad at the top and tapering to a point at its base.

DEER BRUSH

Though its geographic distribution throughout California is similar to that of Buck Brush, you will often find Deer Brush at higher elevations in the mountains—from 1,000 to 7,000 feet in the openings of ponderosa pine or mixed evergreen forests. It is one of the most common *Ceanothus* species in the Sierra Nevada. Also known as Deer Bush, it flourishes in part-shade and tolerates winter freezes.

When compared with Buck Brush, *Ceanothus integerrimus* is a more graceful, relaxed-looking shrub. Its long arching branches, sometimes reaching to 12 or more feet in length, are round and yellow to pale green in color. The bark of the twigs is a similar color and smooth, but the newer twigs are green.

An openly-branched shrub, its pale green leaves—arranged alternate on the stem—sparsely clothe the branches. The oblong- to ovate-shaped leaves are thin and large—up to 3 inches long and half as wide. If the temperature goes too high in mid-summer, Deer Brush, usually winter-deciduous, will shed its leaves early to conserve moisture.

The flowers, arranged in conical clusters at the end of the limber branches, appear from May to July. Borne on 3- to 5-inch-long stems, the flower clusters are up to 6 inches long and 4 inches wide. They are usually white in the Sierra Nevada and blue near the coastal areas; however, they may vary throughout the state from white, to pale or deep blue, and rarely, to pink. Both the flowers and twigs have a sweet, spicy fragrance.

Round to triangular in shape, the three-lobed seed capsule is 1/4 inch or less in width and very viscid or sticky to the touch. Unlike Buck Brush, the capsules of Deer Brush do not have horn-like projections near their tops.

The Native Californians ate the new leaves in spring. Later, they harvested the seeds from the Deer Brush capsules. A decoction made from boiling the root bark in water was taken for coughs and sore throats, and at other times, for malaria and kidney ailments.

The long shoots of Deer Brush supplied material for both coiled and twined baskets. It was commonly used for basket foundations and also in making seed beaters. A lather made from the *Ceanothus* blossoms was used to cleanse the skin and left a clean sweet fragrance.

Ceanothus is from a Greek word meaning "spiny plant". In Latin, *integerrimus* means "absolutely entire"—that is, without teeth and lobes—perhaps referring to the edges of the leaves. Common names include Deer Bush, White Tea-Tree and Soap Bush.

Deer Brush is one of the most important browse plants for California wildlife. In addition, birds and some mammals eat its seed. Deer Brush stump-sprouts after cutting and forms enormous thickets following fires or logging.

BIRCH-LEAF MOUNTAIN-MAHOGANY

Found up to 8,000 feet in the foothills and on the lower mountain slopes of most of California, Birch-Leaf Mountain-Mahogany, *Cercocarpus betuloides* var. *betuloides*, relishes the hot summers of the Far West. Growing in chaparral, dry forests or oak woodlands, Mountain-Mahogany is a large evergreen shrub; it varies from 6 to 26 feet in height. While the young shoots are reddish-brown and covered with hairy down, the scaly bark of the older branches matures to silvery gray.

Arranged alternate on the twigs, the thick, dark green leaves, less than an inch across, are clustered near the tips of the spur-like branches. When first crushed, the young leaves emit a minty fragrance.

The leaves are wedge-shaped, and only the upper half of each leaf margin is toothed. While the undersurface is densely covered with white hairs and woolly in appearance, the upper side is hairless and sticky to the touch. Even more striking are the 5 to 7 prominent veins on the upper leaf surface; it looks as if a special tool has been used to stamp the attractive feather-like pattern.

Unlike several other members of the Rose Family, Mountain-Mahogany has flowers that lack petals. The tiny, 1/4-inch-long sepals are greenish-white in color and are covered with white hairs. Found in clusters of 1 to 12, the fragrant, saucer-like flowers bloom from mid-March to May.

Much more spectacular than the flowers are the unusual, single-seeded fruits, which appear from June to August. Attached to the seed, the flower style lengthens and forms a twisted or curled tail covered with feathery, silver-white hairs. With sunlight reflecting off the 2- to 3- inch-long tails, the whole plant glows. The tails help in wind dispersal of the seeds, but the seeds can also hitchhike to distant places on animal fur.

Though they are botanically unrelated, Mountain-Mahogany and tropical Mahogany (of North and South America) both have dense, red-brown wood with a fine grain. Mountain-Mahogany wood is among the heaviest and hardest woods produced by any of our native plants. Native Californians used it to make clubs, fishing spears, arrowshafts, pipes and even combs. (The combs were made by tying the tiniest twigs together with fiber from the Milkweed plant.)

Native Californians made digging sticks from Mountain-Mahogany by charring one end of a stick in a fire, then scraping it to a fine point on a stone. Digging sticks were used to dig for roots, tubers, bulbs and earthworms in the ground. (Unlike the shovel used by European settlers, the digging sticks of Native Californians removed sought-after items without unearthing large areas or damaging roots, bulbs or plants too small to gather.) To start fires, shorter sticks were used as drills on fire hearths made of California Buckeye or Incense Cedar wood.

The Native Californians made a tea from the inner bark to treat colds or respiratory problems. The inner bark also yielded a purplish dye.

The roots of Mountain-Mahogany serve an important role in stabilizing the soil on hot, dry mountain slopes. Additionally, after a fire, Mountain-Mahogany stump-sprouts, helping to "hold" the barren slope in place during the drenching rains of the next winter season.

Cercocarpus is from the Greek, "kerkos" meaning "tail", and "karpos" meaning "fruit", a reference to the plant's seed. *Betuloides*, meaning "birch-like", alludes to the similarity (seen by some observers) of Mountain-Mahogany leaves to those of the Birch tree, genus *Betula*. In addition to Mountain-Mahogany, other common names include Mountain Ironwood (for its toughness) and Sweet Brush (perhaps for its fragrant flowers).

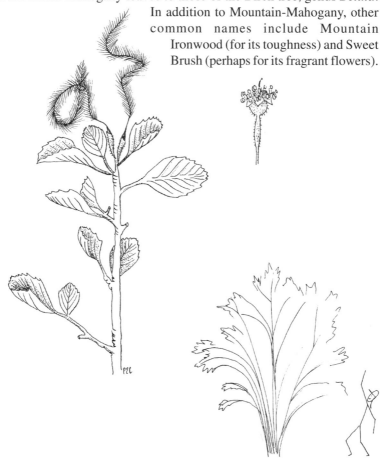

BUSH POPPY

Growing up to 6,000 feet in elevation, Bush Poppy, *Dendromecon rigida*, is found in dry washes and on chaparral slopes in the Coast Ranges from Sonoma County to Baja California, in the mountains of southern California and in the foothills of the Sierra Nevada from Shasta to Tulare Counties. (It is commonly seen in areas of recent wildfires.)

An open, stiffly-branched shrub with stems growing in many directions, Bush Poppy grows to 10 feet in height and 3 to 5 feet in width. Evergreen and glabrous, the plant has yellowish-gray (or, sometimes, nearly white) shreddy bark on its stems and main branches.

Growing sparsely along the stem, the smooth, willow-shaped leaves are arranged alternately on the stem. Stiff, leathery and minutely toothed, they are 1 to 4 inches long and 1/4 to 1 inch wide. The base of the gray-green or blue-green leaves is asymmetrical or uneven. The leaf stalks are twisted, causing the sharp leaf tips to point upward and the flat sides of the leaf to face sideways. This upright orientation tends to keep the plant cooler, since less sun strikes the leaf.

Except for their color, the flowers resemble those of California Poppies. As with California Poppies, the 2 sepals are shed at the time of blossoming. From April to June, the clear yellow, solitary flowers, with 1- to 3-inch stalks, are borne at the end of short branches. The numerous stamens, each topped with an orange anther, add more color. The shiny blossoms have 4 rounded petals—each 3/4 to 1 inch long. They are delicately scented; however, one must linger nearby to take in the essence. This exquisite floral display is fleeting, as the petals drop off soon after pollination.

The fruit—an oblong narrow capsule, 2 to 4 inches long—has many smooth brown or black seeds. Splitting into several pieces, the seed pods curl open from the bottom to the top releasing the seeds.

Though often difficult for the amateur gardener to germinate and bring to flower, Bush Poppy seeds sprout readily—by the thousands—following a wildfire. After germination, heat, full sun and good drainage are essential for the successful development of the seedlings.

The Bush Poppy was discovered in the early 1830s by the plant collector, David Douglas (1799-1834). However, it was not introduced into the horticultural trade until 1854 when William Lobb (1809-1863), a collector for the commercial nursery firm Veitch in England, found some seeds in California. This little-known collector introduced numerous and important species to the nursery trade; he contributed many more species

65

than the better-known Douglas.

Only two species of the genus *Dendromecon* are known anywhere in the world and both of these species are found in California. This genus is rarely found in other western states, though its range does extend to northern Baja California. *Dendromecon*, the only shrub genus in the Poppy Family, means "tree poppy"; *rigida* means "stiff" or "rigid", referring either to the shrub's growth habit or to the stiff, leathery leaves. Other family members include Cream Cups, California Poppy, Matilja Poppy, Prickly Poppy and Bleeding Hearts.

YERBA SANTA

Yerba Santa, *Eriodictyon californicum*, is found in the Great Central Valley and in the foothills of the Sierra Nevada from Kern County northward to Plumas County. It is also found on the lower mountain slopes of the Coast Range from San Luis Obispo north to the Siskiyou and Cascade Ranges, and in Oregon. It thrives on hot, dry slopes of chaparral and in mixed evergreen forests up to 6,000 feet in elevation. A plant of opportunity, it stump-sprouts after fires and grows with renewed vigor following grading, road building or other soil disturbances.

An erect evergreen shrub with shreddy bark, its stems reach to 9 feet high. Yerba Santa normally grows in dense stands as the spreading underground roots send up many shoots. The leaves are arranged alternate on the stem and the twigs are sticky to the touch.

While the undersides of the leaves are woolly, the tops of the dark green leaves, 2 to 6 inches long and less than 2 inches wide, are so thickly covered with a resinous-like substance that they look as if they had been painted or varnished. Some of the older leaves may be black due to a sooty fungus. The willow-shaped, leathery leaves, with their edges rolled under, give off a pungent, yet fresh-smelling fragrance—especially when crushed. (There is great variation in the size and shape of the leaves within its geographic range.)

Appearing from May to July, the buds are held tightly in coiled clusters on one side of the stem; they open one by one as the coil unwinds. The trumpet-shaped flowers, with their 5 fused petals flaring out at the top, are 1/4 to 1/2 inch long. The soft, lilac-colored flowers, sometimes white or pale blue, bloom in profusion at the end of terminal branches; their delicate colors belie the harsh environment. The fruit, a capsule, contains 2 to 20 seeds.

The Native Californians made a dilute beverage by boiling Yerba Santa leaves in water; according to some sources, boiling lessened the bitterness of the leaves. In addition, the fresh leaves were chewed to quench thirst. The leaves tasted bitter at first, but left a sweet aftertaste in the mouth. (It has been reported that early settlers sometimes drank a strong bitter Yerba Santa tea to mask the bitterness of quinine—using bitterness to overcome bitterness.)

Medicinally, Yerba Santa was one of the most important plants used by the Native Californians and has long been revered by them. In the 18th Century, Yerba Santa was also held in high esteem by the early Spanish Californians who learned of its curative powers from the natives.

Native Californians made a strong tea from the leaves to relieve stomachaches, colds, coughs, sore throats and rheumatism. Used externally as a wash, the strong tea solution helped to reduce fever and to soothe sore limbs.

Crushed leaves, in a poultice, were applied to cuts, wounds, insect bites and sprains; a leaf poultice, placed on bone fractures, decreased swelling and pain. A strong aqueous solution prepared from the leaves was used as a lotion to treat poison oak rash.

Because of its curative powers in treating lung ailments, *Eriodictyon californicum* was entered in the U.S. Pharmacopeia from 1894 to 1905 and from 1916 to 1947. It also was listed in the National Formulary from 1826 to 1960.

The genus name, *Eriodictyon*, is derived from two Greek words: "erion" meaning "wool" and "dictyon" meaning "net". "Woolly net" refers to the clusters of fine white hairs found between the veins on the under-sides of the leaves. *Californicum* means "of California".

Yerba Santa means Holy Herb, the common name given to the plant by the Spanish Californians. Other common names are Wild Peach, Mountain Balm, Palo Santa and Consumptive's Weed.

68

NINEBARK

The changing seasons from winter through fall are always a delight, especially as displayed by the deciduous plants. We do not always recognize the subtle differences; however, these plants are constantly reminding us that many things do not stay the same.

And, so it is with Ninebark, *Physocarpus capitatus,* the plant with inflated seed pods. A 3- to 6-foot-high shrub with arching branches, Ninebark can be found on moist stream banks, canyon bottoms or north-facing rocky slopes. Growing up to 4,500 feet in elevation, it is often found in coniferous forests.

Ninebark ranges from northwestern California to the Cascade Range and the Sierra Nevada, then to central and southern California. However, you will not find Ninebark in the Great Central Valley (which includes the Sacramento and San Joaquin Valleys). Out of state, Ninebark extends north to Alaska and east to Utah and Montana.

The new twigs are a reddish color, turning brown as they age. The mature branches of this multi-stemmed shrub have a thin, shreddy, brownish bark that peels off easily. Lewis and Clark called this shrub Sevenbark, because of the many layers of shredding bark. Others have stated that up to twenty layers of the parchment-like bark may peel off. (The number of layers is not confined to seven or nine.) No reference as to the person who named the plant Ninebark was found.

The bright green leaves, 1 to 3 inches long and 3/4 to 1 1/2 inches wide, are maple-shaped with 3 to 5 palmately-veined lobes. The middle lobes are generally much longer and larger than the other ones. The margins of the leaf are usually serrated, with the teeth pointing up toward the leaf tip rather than outward.

From April to June, rose-pink buds appear before the numerous white bell-shaped flowers burst into bloom. At a distance, the flower head, in a rounded terminal cluster on the leafy twigs, resembles a 2-inch white ball. Each of the tiny flowers has 20 to 30 slender stamens that extend well beyond the petals. Each stamen of the newly-opened flowers is tipped with bright red anthers (the pollen-forming portion of the stamen). This "red-speckled" top overshadows the inside of the flower. However, with further aging the stamens collapse, exposing the yellow center of the flower and the developing bladder pods.

Green-colored when immature, the seed pods ripen in July and August becoming a glossy red before fading to a reddish brown. Splitting into a five-pointed dry follicle, each fruit is small, about 1/4 inch wide.

As the season progresses toward fall, Ninebark creates more wondrous sights as its leaves turn to a delicate rose-brown, characteristic of several plants in the Rose Family. After the leaves fall, it displays its shreddy stems and bare twigs—randomly pointing different directions—providing visual interest in an otherwise dull landscape.

At times, the Native Californians ate the seed pods raw. The straightened branches were used to make arrowshafts, while cordage was made from stems that were peeled, then pounded.

Because of the appearance of the fruits, the Greek word, *Physocarpus*, was chosen as the genus name; "physa" means "bladder" and "karpos" means "fruit". *Capitatus* means "having a globular head", referring to the round bouquet of flowers at the tip of the stem. Another common name for *Physocarpus capitatus* is Bridal Wreath, a name also often used for the *Spiraea* of the eastern United States.

A charming shrub to observe throughout the year, Ninebark is worth keeping within our sight.

70

THIMBLEBERRY

Thimbleberry thrives in moist shade from sea level to 8,200 feet in elevation, but it is not found in the Great Central Valley or in the California deserts. At its higher altitudes, the plant is found near the edge of the forest or in more open woods. Outside of California, it ranges north to Alaska; east to Canada, the Rocky Mountains and the Great Lakes; and south to New Mexico and Mexico.

An erect, woody, multi-stemmed shrub, Thimbleberry (*Rubus parviflorus*) grows to 6 feet tall and from 3 to 6 feet wide. Arising from underground rhizomes, many new stems (or canes) sprout each year. The flowers are produced on second-year canes that die back after fruiting. The reddish-brown new bark changes to dark brown, then becomes grayish-brown and shreddy with age—peeling off in thin strips.

The leaves, flowers and fruit of Thimbleberry are displayed in a grandiose style. Perhaps, because it is often found hidden in the shade at the edge of the forest, Thimbleberry dresses up in an exaggerated fashion to draw attention. As an example, the leaves are large—up to 2 to 6 inches wide—with stems almost 5 inches long.

Unlike many species of *Rubus*, the leaves of Thimbleberry are simple (not compound); in addition, they are maple-like and five-lobed. Arranged alternate on the stem, they have conspicuous palmate veins arising from their heart-shaped bases; the leaf margins are coarsely and irregularly toothed. Green on both surfaces, the leaves are soft to the touch. On hot days, they give off a pleasant fragrance, especially when crushed. In the fall, the leaves turn to a soft yellow before dropping. Of the several *Rubus* species native to California, *parviflorus* is one of three species that is unarmed—its stems and leaves have no prickles or spines.

Equally impressive, the large white blossoms, up to 2 inches across, are crimped and similar in appearance to crepe paper flowers. In terminal clusters of 4 to 7, the delicately fragrant flowers bloom from April to June. Numerous yellow stamens and pistils are crowded into the center of the rose-like flower. Each of the 5 rounded petals is turned in a bit to form a wide saucer.

Another unusual feature of Thimbleberry is the large, red to dark scarlet, sweet-perfumed fruit; it is about 1/2 to 3/4 inches wide and 3/4 inches long. The immature fruit is firmly attached and will not fall off; when ripe, the raspberry-like fruits separate easily from the receptacle—the "platter" on which the flower, then later the fruit, rests. In shape, the berry appears to be an upside-down bowl or perhaps a wide thimble—

hence the origin of the common name, Thimbleberry.

Botanically speaking, the fruit is a group of drupelets (small drupes) formed around a central core; each drupelet has its own stone. These stones are the "seeds" that catch between the teeth when one eats various kinds of berries.

Native Californians ate the tender shoots of Thimbleberry either fresh or boiled. In addition, some natives ate the berries raw, while others dried the fruit, then pounded it to a mealy consistency to be mixed with dried meat or fish. This mixture, pemmican, was shaped into cakes to eat later when traveling.

Native Californians drank teas made from *Rubus* leaves for diarrhea and to treat indigestion. An aqueous extract of the Thimbleberry root was taken as a tonic to stimulate poor appetites.

Rubus, an ancient Latin name for "bramble", originated from the word "ruber", meaning "red"—a possible connection with the bright color of bramble berries and their juice.

In botanical Latin, the species name often describes some attribute of a specific plant. Perhaps the person who named this species was a non-conformist choosing to confuse plant followers? *Parviflorus* means "small-flowered", but *R. parviflorus* has the largest flowers (sometimes more than 2 inches across) of any species in the *Rubus* genus!

BLUE ELDERBERRY

Blue Elderberry grows along stream banks and open areas of forests in all of California up to 10,000 feet in elevation, except in the Colorado, Sonoran and Mojave Deserts. It extends north to western Canada, east to Utah and south to New Mexico and Mexico.

A multi-stemmed shrub—lacking a main trunk—Blue Elderberry (*Sambucus mexicana*) varies from 6 to 25 feet tall, generally having a similar width. However, it is most often found about 10 to 15 feet tall. Growing in thickets, the shrub has a round to flat crown; from a distance, it resembles a miniature mushroom cloud.

The odd-pinnately compound leaves, 5 to 8 inches long, are arranged opposite on the branches. The leaves, thick and dark green, tend to arch out, then downward from the stems. The 3 to 9 finely-toothed leaflets are also arranged opposite on the leaf stem—the "odd" leaflet is attached at the tip of the leaf. Varying from 1 to 8 inches in length, the tips of the oblong- to ovate-shaped leaflets are acute or pointed. The bases of the leaflets are attached with little or no stem. Deciduous in winter, the leaves turn a clear yellow in fall.

Depending on the elevation, myriads of tiny, 1/4-inch-wide, creamy-white flowers burst forth from April to August. Arranged in flat-topped clusters, 2 to 13 inches wide, the five-petalled flowers form a delicate lacy pattern reminding some of the doilies of olden days. At twilight, the light-colored flowers release a strong bouquet (or scent) to attract night-pollinating insects; Elderberry blossoms provide a rich nectar source.

The blue-black or black berries (actually drupes), 1/4 inch in diameter, are covered with a whitish waxy film that causes them to appear more bluish in color. (Interestingly enough, some members of the 1804-1806 Lewis and Clark Expedition described this shrub as an elder with sky-blue berries.)

Only the flowers and the berries of *Sambucus mexicana* were eaten by the Native Californians. They always cooked or dried the berries from *S. mexicana* before eating as the freshly harvested fruit often caused nausea. A limited quantity of cooked berries was eaten in season, so that a larger portion could be dried and saved for winter use. (The berries of *Sambucus racemosa*, Red Elderberry, are considered poisonous.)

The genus *Sambucus* (including Blue Elderberry and Red Elderberry) was used medicinally by many tribes in California. "Teas" made from the blossoms were used for many purposes: to cleanse the skin, to medicate eye infections, to lessen swelling from sprains and bruises and to relieve

73

cold symptoms. Taken internally, the "teas" were especially efficient in the treatment of chills and fever as the "teas" caused excessive perspiration, thereby alleviating some of the symptoms. (The roots, bark, leaves and stems of ALL Elderberry species are toxic.)

Native Californians prepared a black or purple dye from the fruit and twigs of the Blue Elderberry to color basketry materials. Fresh leaves were boiled in water to make a light green or yellowish dye.

Native Californians called Elderberry, "The Tree of Music". They made flutes and musical bows, as well as split-stick clapper rattles and whistles, from elder branches that had been gathered the previous spring and then dried. Only the flute and musical bow were capable of producing melodies—the other instruments were used to provide a tempo or beat.

Native Californians often trimmed back Elderberry shrubs in the fall to obtain long straight new branches the following spring. To remove the pith in the center, they bored a hole in the stem with a hot stick. Elder wood was also used to make arrowshafts and hunting bows.

Sambucus is from the Greek word, "sambuke", a flute-like instrument made from elder wood; *mexicana* means "native to Mexico". In folklore of long ago, Elderberry shrubs were reputed to possess magical powers and these bushes were often planted near houses with hopes of keeping evil spirits away.

Caution: The roots, bark, leaves and stems of ALL Elderberry species are toxic. (The berries of Red Elderberry are also considered poisonous.)

74

RED ELDERBERRY

Red Elderberry (*Sambucus racemosa* var. *racemosa*) prospers in moist places, as does Blue Elderberry, but it is not found in the Great Basin or in the Great Central Valley of California. Its growing range extends from 6,000 feet to 11,000 feet in elevation—slightly higher than that for *Sambucus mexicana*.

A bit shorter than *S. mexicana*, the maximum height of Red Elderberry approaches 20 feet, yet it is more commonly found about 6 feet high. The pith of its branches is more brownish than that of the Blue Elderberry.

The leaves are odd-pinnately compound, the same as those of Blue Elderberry, and are arranged opposite on the branches. Both the thin leaves and the leaflets of *S. racemosa* var. *racemosa* are shorter than those of Blue Elderberry. The leaves of Red Elderberry are 3 to 6 inches long; the leaflets are almost the same length.

With 5 to 7 leaflets, Red Elderberry has less variation in the number of leaflets than does Blue Elderberry (which has 3 to 9). The ovate to elliptic leaflets of Red Elderberry are sharply toothed as compared with the finely serrated leaflets of Blue Elderberry.

However, the above-listed differences between the species are minor; it would take careful observation for an amateur to identify the plants without blooms or berries.

There are three major differences between the species: the time of blooming, the shape and size of the inflorescence (the flower cluster) and the color of the berries.

The cream-colored flowers are equally small in each of the Elderberry shrubs. Blooming from May to July, the blossoms of Red Elderberry are arranged in dome-shaped or pyramidal clusters (each 2 1/2 to 4 inches long), rather than in the flat-topped clusters of Blue Elderberry.

When ripe, the berries of *Sambucus racemosa* var. *racemosa* are bright red, sometimes black, and about the same size as those of *S. mexicana*. Lacking the waxy white film of Blue Elderberry, the berries of Red Elderberry are very attractive with their accompanying bright green foliage. The berries of both species are relished by birds and mammals.

Sambucus is from the Greek word, "sambuke", for a musical instrument made from the elder wood. *Racemosa* (from the species and variety names) is derived from the Latin word, "racemose", meaning "having racemes". A raceme is a cluster of flowers each of which is singly borne on a short stalk attached to the main plant stem, generally in an upright position. The flowers bloom successively from the bottom to the top. However, in this case, "having racemes" may loosely refer to the upright, elongated dome-shaped flower cluster that blooms from the bottom to the top of the main stem.

The medicinal, musical and horticultural uses that Native Californians made of this plant are described under Blue Elderberry.

Caution: The berries of Red Elderberry are considered poisonous to humans and the Native Californians did NOT eat them. In addition, the roots, stems and leaves of ALL Elderberry species are poisonous.

AMERICAN DOGWOOD

As its common name suggests, American Dogwood (*Cornus sericea*) grows over a vast geographic area of North America: from Alaska south to northern Mexico and eastward across Canada to Labrador and Newfoundland. Except for in the deserts, look for American Dogwood along creeks or stream banks, near willow thickets or in boggy meadows below 9,200 feet in elevation all over California. American Dogwood prefers partial shade and is often found as an understory shrub in the ponderosa pine forest on the western slope of the Sierra. Its affinity for moisture is evident from another common name, Creek Dogwood.

A multi-stemmed, rounded shrub, American Dogwood may grow to over 13 feet, although it usually reaches no more than 6 to 8 feet. Forming a dense thicket, it readily roots aboveground where the stems touch the soil. It also forms suckers from underground stems, or rhizomes, making it an excellent plant for erosion control near waterways. While the bark of the older branches is grayish-green, the bark of the new twigs is bright purplish-red, eliciting other common names: Red-twigged Dogwood, Red-osier Dogwood and Red Willow.

Arranged opposite on the stem, the egg-shaped leaves, 2 to 4 inches long, are bright green and smooth above, paler with fine white hairs beneath. The leaf edges are entire, not toothed, and the leaf tips are sharp.

A distinguishing feature of the genus *Cornus* is its deeply veined

leaves. *Cornus sericea* has 4 to 7 pairs of sunken veins radiating out from the mid-vein of the leaf. Then in a somewhat parallel fashion, they curve upward toward the leaf tip. These cavernous furrows resemble the contour rows of a plowed field. The leaves are deciduous and provide a brilliant display in the fall when the leaf colors range from tannish-pink to crimson to purple-red.

Arranged in flat-topped cymes, the white- to cream-colored flowers bloom from April to November. Located at the tips of the branches, the flower cluster is 1 1/2 to 2 inches across. Look closely at each tiny 1/8-inch star-like flower to see its 4 white petals and its 4 stamens showing off their yellow anthers.

The flowers of American Dogwood lack the showy white petal-like bracts associated with two species of *Cornus*: the ground-hugging Bunchberry and the tree-like Mountain Dogwood.

Maturing in late summer, each globe-shaped fruit is a 1/4- to 1/3-inch drupe; it has a smooth stone enclosing 2 seeds. Often, American Dogwood and other members of this genus bear two crops of flowers and berries. In the fall, the white berries contrasted with the reddish-purple leaves delight our senses.

Native Californians ate the fruit, though it was considered bitter by some. They harvested the sturdy stems of this species to make cradleboards for their infants; stems were also used as a basketry material. The thin, pliable branches were made into thick cordage or rope. An aqueous extract, obtained by boiling the dried roots or bark, was used as a tonic. (The inner bark of *Cornus* has some of the properties of quinine.)

The genus name is derived from the Latin "cornu" meaning "horn"— a reference to the hardness of the wood. The species name, *sericea*, means "silky" or "with long straight close-pressed glossy hairs" perhaps a reference to the "fine white hairs" on the underside of the leaf.

SERVICE-BERRY

Ranging from 200 to almost 9,000 feet in elevation, *Amelanchier alnifolia* (Service-Berry) grows in moist places in the Sierra Nevada and the North Coast Ranges. It extends up to Alaska and east to the Rockies, Arizona and New Mexico. It is also found in all of the most northerly states between the Pacific and the Atlantic Oceans.

Usually a tall shrub, this multi-branched plant varies from 3 to 15 feet in height and is about 4 to 6 feet in width. Erect in habit, its stiffly-spreading branches are reddish-brown when young, changing to a grayish-brown with age. The stems are slender and generally smooth. In the wild, one often finds this shrub growing in thickets, a solid mass of ascending branches.

The simple leaves, arranged alternate on the stem, are oval to roundish in shape. About 3/4 to 2 inches long and 1/2 to 1 3/4 inches wide, the leaves are one-veined from their rounded or slightly heart-shaped bases. On the free end of the leaf, the margins are distinctively toothed—but only from the middle of the leaf to its tip. The dark blue-green leaves with paler gray-green undersides are soft to the touch. In the fall, the leaves turn a bright golden yellow before dropping.

The flowers of Service-Berry are borne in compact clusters, 1 to 2 inches wide, at the end of the short lateral (side) twigs. Each cluster is made up of 2 to 6 flowers; rarely does one see a solitary flower at the tip of a twig. The 5 erect petals of Service-Berry are unique: they are crinkly, strap-shaped, slightly twisted, and much longer than wide. The petals are about 1/2 to 3/4 inch long. As is characteristic of many members of the Rose Family, Service-Berry has numerous stamens—up to 20. When in bloom in May or June, this shrub is most conspicuous as the white flower clusters cover the entire bush before it leafs out. The petals fall early, so the spectacle is short-lived.

Berry-like pomes, bluish-purple to purplish-black, appear in June and July. The persistent fruit is round and about 1/2 inch in diameter, with small seeds inside. (Pomes, like the fruit of an apple, have the seeds enclosed in fleshy pulp, while the fruit of a many-seeded berry has no central core.) When you find one in the wild, notice the base of the fruit with the dried remnants of its flower calyx; you'll see that it's similar to the calyx of an apple.

Service-Berry was valuable to the Native Californians. The berries were a significant food source, eaten fresh or dried for future use. From the dried berries, they made pemmican—a high-calorie food to carry when traveling.

Some tribes used the straight, slender shoots for arrowshafts, while others formed foreshafts from the wood; these were then attached to arrowshafts or to salmon harpoons. In basket making, Service-Berry twigs and stems were frequently interwoven to stiffen baskets or to reinforce the rims of those baskets used in carrying heavy loads. Baby carriers were also fashioned from the *Amelanchier* wood.

In addition, an eyewash was prepared by boiling the green inner bark. The crushed berries yielded a dark dye.

Within its range, Service-Berry has numerous common names: in New England, Shadbush, because it blooms in the season of the annual run of the shad; in the Midwest, June Berry, for the time of year the fruit ripens; in western Canada, Saskatoon, a Native American name; and Mountain Pear, by Far West explorers.

Service, the first part of the often-used common name Service-Berry, may be an altered form of the old botanical name, *Sorbus*, which was formerly applied to this genus. Many old-timers, long since departed, insisted that Service-Berry be pronounced "Sarvis-Berry"—the "sar" rhyming with "jar".

The genus name, *Amelanchier*, is from the Latin form of the French common name, and the species name, *alnifolia*, means "with alder-like leaves".

Service-Berry is an important browse plant for wildlife.

80

FLANNELBUSH

Except in desert areas, Flannelbush (*Fremontodendron californicum*) is found throughout California. Growing at elevations between 1,300 and 6,600 feet, it is most commonly found in chaparral and oak-pine woodlands.

Flannelbush prospers on the western slopes of the Sierra Nevada from Kern County north to Tehama County; in scattered places in the Inner and Middle Coast Ranges from Lake County south to San Luis Obispo; and on dry canyon slopes of the Tehachapi and San Jacinto Mountains and the Transverse Range in southern California. It extends east to Arizona and south to Baja California.

Maturing rapidly from 6 to 16 feet high and from 4 to 6 feet wide, Flannelbush has a rounded or open crown of wide-spreading branches; these branches are tough, flexible and covered with dense hairs. When several of these plants grow side by side, the lower branches form an impenetrable thicket. The young twigs are densely covered with rust-colored hairs. With age, the outer bark becomes smooth and turns a red-brown color. (In times past, the flexible smaller branches were used for whips by teamsters.)

Often appearing on spur shoots, the oval- to round-shaped evergreen leaves (1/3 to 2 inches wide) are arranged alternate on the stem. Somewhat resembling maple leaves, these simple leaves are often palmately to pinnately lobed. The upper sides of the leathery leaves are dark green with rusty-brown edges, while the undersides are dull green and coated with dense gray or white bristly hairs.

Blooming in May or June, *Fremontodendron* has a solitary flower made of 5 petal-like sepals united at their bases. (Flannelbush has no petals.) Having short stems, the flowers are often found on the stubby spur shoots. A clear lemon yellow, they are saucer-shaped and 1 1/2 to 2 1/2 inches across. Tending to bloom all at once, the blossoms last about two weeks. After the flowers dry up, they persist on the stems—later developing into oval-shaped capsules with dense, stiff, straight hairs. The brown seed capsules, 3/4 to 1 1/2 inches in diameter, open from the top to reveal 2 or 3 brown seeds inside.

The Native Californians found many uses for this beautiful, but bristly, plant. Fiber from the outer bark was made into cordage and sometimes also used as bow string. Smaller branches were used to make arrows, while bows were fashioned from larger ones.

For medicinal purposes, a tea was brewed from the bark to relieve throat irritations. The inner bark, gelatinous and soothing, was used to poultice sores.

Fremontodendron was named for General John C. Fremont (1813-1890) who discovered the plant in 1846 on his 3rd expedition to the Far West. He was an officer in the U. S. Topographical Corps and the purpose of the expeditions was to revise or make new maps of the territories they passed through. Additionally, he made many botanical observations and was a zealous plant collector on his various journeys.

Flannelbush provides a protective covering for dry foothill slopes and readily sprouts following wildfires or other damage. Though considered to be an evergreen plant, Flannelbush will shed some of its leaves to conserve moisture during droughty times. Then, after the winter rains, it bursts forth with new leaves.

"Dendron" is the Greek word meaning "tree". The species name, *californicum*, means "of California". This is one of two *Fremontodendron* species native to California. Started from seeds, *F. californicum* has been in cultivation in England since the mid-1850s. The common name, Flannelbush, may originate from the very dense, stiff hairs that cover the stems, twigs and back sides of the leaves, which gives an appearance of tannish-colored flannel. However, don't confuse the look of "flannel" with its actual softness. The hairs can irritate the skin.

Other common names include Silver Oak, Leatherwood and California Slippery Elm.

When in blossom, Flannelbush is truly a handsome shrub with its abundance of conspicuous yellow flowers. It is often included in plant lists as one of the best native shrubs for use in public or private landscapes.

Caution: Flannelbush's deciduous hairs, while not poisonous, can irritate the skin—and are to be avoided. (Always protect yourself when working around this plant).

SNOWBERRY

A charming plant, Snowberry (*Symphoricarpos albus* var. *laevigatus*) draws back from the sunlight to retire into comfortable shade; it grows below 4,000 feet in elevation on the north slopes of canyon areas or near streams in forests and woodlands in the coastal mountain ranges and in the Sierra Nevada foothills. It occurs north to Alaska and east to Montana and Wyoming.

A multi-stemmed shrub, up to 6 feet tall, Snowberry eventually forms large colonies or thickets from its everspreading underground rhizomes. The slender stems of this deciduous shrub are stiff and generally upright, though occasionally some branch to the side. The bark of the young twigs is thin and light brown. Later, with aging, it becomes shreddy with a gray or dark brown color.

The leaves on the new shoots, up to 2 1/2 inches wide, are larger than those on the older wood. On the older branches, the pale green leaves, arranged opposite on the stems, are ovate to almost round and up to 1 1/4 inches in diameter. A unique and consistent feature of the leaves is their lack of uniformity: the edges of the leaves may be even or uneven, toothed or untoothed, shallowly lobed or not lobed at all. Additionally, some of the leaves appear as though they have been browsed by an animal, leaving a large portion missing.

Eight to sixteen flowers are clustered in the leaf axil or at the end of the stems; each of the tiny, pinkish, bell-shaped flowers is 1/8 to 1/4 inch long. Blooming in May and June, the drooping, five-lobed blossoms are hidden by the new foliage; they are rarely noticed, unless you chance upon a strongly fragrant plant. Seek them out—the sweet scent is delightful.

In late summer or fall, clusters of the pulpy, round berries, about 1/2 inch in diameter, follow the flowers. Long after the leaves have fallen, the berries persist. Well into the cold, drab days of winter, they provide a bit of cheer in contrast to the seemingly dead plant. Usually, Snowberry does not lose all of its berries until the plant leafs out the next spring. The common name, Snowberry, may have originated from the clusters of snow-white berries which, from a distance, could lead one to imagine that the bare branches are covered with scattered clumps of snow. (Or perhaps it was just named for the snow-colored berries?)

The two-seeded berries are variously described as insipid, tasteless, spongy, inedible and even poisonous. It has been reported that ingestion of the berries of Snowberry can cause severe intestinal distress. Therefore, it seems sensible to leave the berries to the birds and other wildlife. In fact, some authors maintain that the berries may even be poisonous to animals, since they remain on the bush for such a long time; others say this is not so.

The Native Californians pounded the roots, then made a tea to treat colds and stomachaches. Some tribes used the plant stem, slender and pithy, for pipe stems.

The genus name, *Symphoricarpos*, is derived from the Greek: "symphoreo" means "to bear together", while "karpos" means "fruit"; together, these refer to the profusion of berries. The species name, *albus*, means "white", suggesting the color of the berries; *laevigatus*, means "smooth and polished", which might indicate that the berries are hairless.

Snowberry was first collected by Pedr Kalm (1715-1779), a Swedish collector working in eastern North America. The Swedish botanist Linnaeus named *Kalmia*, a handsome plant from the Heath Family, for him.

Caution: Ingestion of the berries of Snowberry may cause severe intestinal distress.

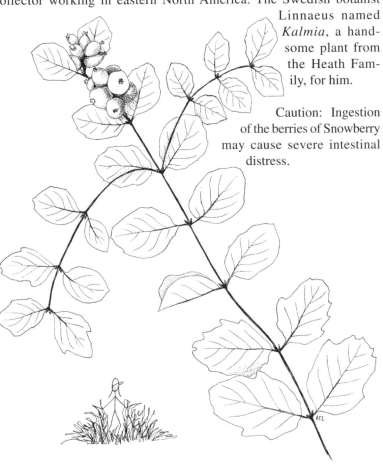

SPICEBUSH

Calycanthus occidentalis, Spicebush, is endemic to California, meaning that it is confined solely within its geographical borders. The only other species of *Calycanthus* in North America prospers in the warm, moist climate of southeastern United States. Though widely separated from the eastern *Calycanthus*, the tropical appearance of *Calycanthus occidentalis* and its affinity for moisture suggests that it might be a survivor from times past when the California summers were wetter and milder.

Spicebush is found in the Inner and Outer North Coast Ranges from Sonoma and Napa Counties north to Trinity County; in the Sierra Nevada foothills; and in the central and southern Sierra Nevada from Tuolumne County south to Kern County. Occurring below 5,000 feet in elevation, Spicebush thrives in moist shady places, along streams and in canyons. It is intolerant of prolonged cold or late spring frosts.

A rounded, multi-trunked shrub, it grows from 3 1/2 to 10 feet tall and is almost as wide. The brown, shreddy bark and the crushed leaves and twigs have a sweet, spicy fragrance, similar to nutmeg, allspice or cloves. Undoubtedly, this scent suggested the common name, Spicebush.

The rich green leaves vary from 1 1/4 to 6 inches long and are about half as wide. Arranged opposite on the stem, they are ovate or oblong in shape with one main vein arising from the base. The base of the leaf is rounded or heart-shaped; the tip tapers to a sharp point. While the underleaf surface is hairy, the upper leaf surface is rough to the touch, but hairless. The leaves turn a soft yellow color before falling.

From May to July, the solitary, 2-inch-wide flowers appear at the ends of the branches. The 1-inch-long sepals and petals of this chrysanthemum-like flower are numerous, and they last only a day or two. To this author, the flowers are a beautiful maroon-red, yet some others describe the color of the blossoms as reddish-brown, wine-colored or wine-red.

Sensations and emotions elicited from various smells are an individual matter. There are few native shrubs whose foliage or flowers bring forth such diverse and strong responses as does Spicebush. The choice of words used to describe the sense of smell gives some insight as to our likes and dislikes. The words "perfume", "aroma" or "fragrance" often connote an agreeable, attractive, sweet or pleasing smell. However, "odor", and sometimes "smell" or "scent", may suggest an undesirable or negative impression.

There was general agreement among various authors regarding the aromatic fragrance or pleasant aroma of the bark, and the crushed leaves and twigs. But these same plant-people had very different descriptions of the flower's smell: "unpleasant odor", "not a sweet shrub", "winy", "not sweet", "wine-like fragrance" and finally, "odors of strawberries or wine or vinegar". Nevertheless, beetles—the pollinators of the Spicebush flower—are attracted by this unusual scent and life goes on.

The beige-colored fruit—a woody urn- or cup-shaped receptacle— is heavily veined and about an inch long. It contains numerous brownish achenes (or seeds) and the fruit persists on the shrub until the next season's flowers appear.

The Native Californians made a tea from the bark of Spicebush to treat the symptoms of colds, sore throats and stomachaches. They also worked the Spicebush wood into arrowshafts.

The genus name, *Calycanthus,* is derived from a Greek word, "kalyx" meaning "calyx or bud covering", and "antho", meaning "a flower"— describing the cup-shaped hollow fruit. The species name, *occidentale,* means "western", denoting Spicebush's geographic origin. Other common names for this shrub include Wine Flower, Vinegar Bush, Sweet-Shrub, Strawberry Bush and California Calycantha.

Spicebush was introduced into cultivation in 1831 from seed collected by David Douglas (1799-1834).

86

MOUNTAIN MISERY

Mountain Misery, *Chamaebatia foliolosa*, grows only in the coniferous forests on the western slopes of the Sierra Nevada from Kern County to Sierra County and in the Cascade Mountains. Between 1,900 and 7,200 feet in elevation, you will find solid carpets of Mountain Misery on the forest floor beneath ponderosa pines, firs and sometimes lodgepole pines. It is tolerant of snow and cold in the high mountains, withstands the summer heat of the lower foothills and prospers in dry shade.

A low, woody, evergreen shrub, from 8 inches to 2 feet high, Mountain Misery forms a soft, dull-green ground cover. Multi-branched, the bark on the stems is smooth and dark brown.

The attractive fern-like leaves are arranged alternate and clustered near the end of the stem. Each leaf is up to 4 inches long and ovate or oblong in outline. The odd-pinnate leaflets, usually divided two or three times into crowded segments, are elliptical in shape. On hot summer days, the sticky resin of the foliage gives off a strong medicinal-like odor, liked by some, but detested by many.

Blooming from May to July, the single flowers are arranged in 1- to 2-inch-long, flat-topped clusters at the end of the stems. Each strawberry-like flower has 5 white 1/2-inch-wide petals and numerous yellow stamens. The leathery fruit, an achene, is enclosed in the dry calyx.

Mountain Misery was used by the Native Californians for various purposes. Only those who understood the details of preparation would use Mountain Misery leaves in a medicinal decoction. The tea, consumed while still hot, was taken for rheumatism and for diseases that had skin eruptions, such as chicken pox, measles and smallpox. (These skin diseases were never treated by the shaman.) They also drank leaf teas for relief from coughs and colds. At times, other herbs were added to the brewing Mountain Misery leaves.

The genus name, *Chamaebatia*, is derived from two Greek words: "chamae" meaning "on the ground" and "batos" for "bramble"; the name describes a "low-growing bramble". *Foliolosa* in Latin means "full of leaves" or "many-leaved", probably referring to the excessively leafy shrub. Other common names include Bear Mat, Running-Oak and Bear Clover; the Native Californians called the plant Kit-kit-dizze.

Mountain Misery is not a popular shrub with many people due to its strong, volatile scent, its perceived flammability and its invasive roots. However, by creating thick matted carpets, Mountain Misery effectively eliminates the growth of most seedlings, perennials and annuals in the coniferous forest, thereby reducing the amount of underbrush fuel.

In addition, the extensive underground network of stems and roots of Mountain Misery stabilizes the soil on steep slopes and aids in erosion control. (It sprouts quickly after a wildfire and its dull green carpet can be re-established within two years after a fire.) The leaves and stems are browsed by deer, sheep and goats.

Though distressing to some, the scent of Mountain Misery leaves reminds me of many pleasurable hours spent in the mountains with the warm wind gently wafting fragrances from the forests.

CREAM BUSH

There are five species of *Holodiscus* in the Americas, two of which are native to California: *H. discolor* and *H. microphyllus*. *Holodiscus discolor*, Cream Bush, has 3/4- to 1 1/2-inch elliptical leaves on its peg-like stems; on its other stems, the leaves are 3/4 to 4 3/4 inches long and egg-shaped. The leaves of Cream Bush are coarsely toothed or scalloped from the middle of the leaf to the leaf tip. There are no leaves in the terminal floral cluster.

(In contrast, *Holodiscus microphyllus*, Rock-Spiraea, has smaller leaves, up to 3/4 inches long, on peg-like stems; the leaves are obovate in shape. On its other stems, the leaves are up to 1 inch long and round to oval-shaped. The leaves of Rock Spiraea may be scalloped or toothed and they are intermingled in the terminal floral cluster. Additionally, within each species, there are great variations in several leaf characteristics, including leaf size, leaf shape and extent of hairiness.)

Though Cream Bush prefers the part-shade of moist woodlands, damp canyons or north-facing slopes, one will also find it on rocky ledges on the coast from Del Norte County to the San Francisco Bay area. It also grows up to 6,000 feet in elevation in the mountain ranges of northwestern California and in the Sierra Nevada, and below 4,000 feet in the central and southern California mountains. As Cream Bush sprouts in open or disturbed land, you will often find it in logged-over areas, in second-growth forests and at road banks.

While Cream Bush may reach only 5 feet in height in drier, mountainous terrain, it may grow to 20 feet in coastal regions. However, this erect, multi-stemmed shrub with long arching branches is more commonly found growing to 10 or 12 feet. Its stems are often hairy and thin sheets of bark can be peeled off the older gray branches.

The deciduous leaves are arranged alternate on the short lateral, reddish-colored twigs. The upper side of the leaf is a pale, gray-green. The underside is covered with soft, white woolly hairs and the leaves are soft and fuzzy to the touch, similar to those of Mountain-Mahogany. Thick, pinnate veins arising from the sides of the midrib conspicuously mark the lower surface of the leaf. Though the leaves turn to a beautiful deep orange-yellow before they drop, the show is not spectacular because the leaves are too small to make a big splash.

At the ends of the stems, the 2 1/2- to 10-inch-long pyramidal flower clusters consist of a profusion of 1/8-inch rose-like flowers. Blooming from May to July, the flowers have 5 petals and 15 to 20 stamens. The long stamens that extend well beyond the petals create a light, airy feeling and, with imagination, the illusion of a bubbly, foamy, floral spray. Near the ocean, this shrub is called Oceanspray.

The buds, a light pink, open to creamy-white blossoms that fade, with age, to a yellowish- or rusty-brown. The fruit, a dry brown capsule about 1/8 inch wide, is hairy and one-seeded. The dried flowers and seeds persist on the plant over the winter.

The flowers and the crushed leaves often exude a delicious perfume. You must get close to the flowers to enjoy this fruity odor, which is similar to that of some fruit-flavored chewing gums. Unfortunately, not every flower spray has this delightful sweet-smelling fragrance. This aroma may well be the origin of another common name, Meadow Sweet. Volatile oils are usually responsible for these flower scents, which are attractants for pollinators, especially moths, but also for bees and butterflies.

The Native Californians sometimes ate the small fruits. They made arrowshafts from the long straight branches and also used the wood to make gambling sticks. Another common name, Indian Arrow Wood, may have been derived, perhaps, from the use of *Holodiscus* wood.

Holodiscus, from the Greek words "holos" meaning "whole" and "diskos" meaning "disc", refers to the unlobed receptacle or disc beneath the petals. *Discolor*, means "of different, but not necessarily only two, colors", perhaps referring to the leaves.

Holodiscus discolor was one of several plants discovered on the 1804-1806 Lewis and Clark Expedition.

WILD MOCK ORANGE

It is not too surprising that Lewis and Clark, on their 1804-1806 expedition to Oregon, would recognize a new species of *Philadelphus* in the Far West; the genus, *Philadelphus*, had a widespread distribution in their home region of the eastern United States. In California, you will discover *P. lewisii* growing on slopes, in forest openings or in canyons up to 5,000 feet in elevation.

Nowhere abundant, Wild Mock Orange usually is seen as a single specimen along the North Coast; in the Klamath, North Coast and Cascade Ranges; and in the Sierra Nevada. Outside California, it extends northward to British Columbia and eastward to Montana.

A loosely-branched, multi-stemmed shrub, Wild Mock Orange grows up to 10 feet tall and almost as wide, assuming an overall rounded shape. The stems are long and straight and arranged opposite on the branches. The bark on the new young shoots is reddish and smooth; with aging, it turns gray and becomes shreddy—either peeling off in strips or in rectangular patches.

With 3 prominent veins from each base, the leaves are arranged opposite on the stems. The leaf surfaces usually are hairless and the margins are entire—having no teeth or indentations. The ovate leaves are 1 1/4 to 3 1/2 inches long and 3/4 to 1 1/2 inches wide; they are light green above and paler beneath. Between plants, there is great variability in leaf size, smoothness of leaf margins and hairiness.

Mock Orange draws little attention to itself when not in bloom as it blends in with other shrubs whether in green leaf in spring or leafless in winter. But it is the showy flowers that make this shrub so spectacular. From May to July, six or more white flowers in a cluster appear at the end of the stems. The single, rose-like flowers are about an inch across. Each of the four-petalled flowers is decorated with 20 to 40 creamy-yellow stamens and 1 green pistil. At times, the shrub is almost covered with blossoms.

This is a flower to linger near. Its fragrance is delightful, variously described as a clean-scented bouquet, or as a pineapple- or citrus-like perfume. No mention of the origin of the common name, Mock Orange, was found. Could it have resulted from the citrusy scent of the flowers? Another member of the Mock Orange Family, *Carpenteria*, also has white fragrant flowers, but they are not as heavily scented as those of Wild Mock Orange.

The fruit, a 3/8-inch-wide woody capsule, is widest in the middle and tapers at each end. It is divided into 5 parts, each containing numerous brown seeds.

The Native Californians made arrowshafts, pipe stems and combs from the straight stem branches. The older, less pithy wood was used to make bows. The leaves and bark of Mock Orange made suds in water and served as a cleanser.

The genus, *Philadelphus*, was named after Ptolemy II Philadelphus, (309-247 B.C.), a Greek king of ancient Egypt and a patron of the arts and sciences. In Greek, "philos" means "beloved" and "adelphos" means "brother"; together they mean "loving brother". This author could find no explanation as to why this shrub should be so remembered. However, Mock Orange has long been associated with love, and bouquets of these flowers were prominent at summer weddings in early America.

Obviously, the species name, *lewisii*, is after Captain Meriwether Lewis, who discovered it in 1804. Wild Mock Orange is sometimes called Syringa, and it is by this common name that the state of Idaho has recognized it as their state flower. It was introduced to England in 1825 by David Douglas (1799-1834).

This is another California plant that sprouts readily after fires. Also, it is browsed by deer and elk, and its seeds are eaten by quail.

PEC

92

WESTERN AZALEA

Have you ever been hiking along a streamside trail when suddenly you get a whiff of a delightful spicy fragrance, perhaps similar to nutmeg? After your first encounter, you know immediately that somewhere nearby, Western Azaleas are in bloom. Western Azalea, *Rhododendron occidentale*, grows near sea level along the North and Central Coasts down to Santa Barbara. It is found up to 7,200 feet in elevation in the Klamath, Cascade, North Coast and Central Coast Ranges; in the Sierra Nevada; and in the Inner Coast Range and San Jacinto Mountains of southern California.

Growing along stream banks, near springs and in moist coniferous forests, Western Azalea is a member of the wonderful Heath Family—the same family to which the drought-tolerant Manzanitas, the Snow Plants of the deep forests and the alpine Heathers of the high country belong.

An erect, multi-stemmed and densely branched shrub, Western Azalea is usually found about 8 to 10 feet tall, though it can vary from 3 to 15 feet in height. It is often as wide as it is tall. The bark of the slender twigs is shreddy.

Western Azalea offers many visual treats from spring into fall. Emerging in spring, the thin, deciduous leaves, clustered at the ends of the twigs, are a bright green. Later in the season, the leaves gradually darken, adding a bit of purple or brown to their green color. But the color climax is reached in fall when the leaves put on a glorious, colorful display—crimson, scarlet, yellow or gold—depending on many factors, including the plant's color genes.

The upper leaf surface is glabrous—without hairs—but the light green underside may be either hairless or covered with fine hairs. The leaf margins have short, straight hairs. The simple leaves, elliptical in shape, are 1 1/4 to 3 1/2 inches long and 1/2 to 1 1/4 inches wide. The leaf tips have broad points.

Blooming from May to July, the flowers fill the air with a spicy fragrance, sweet and nutmeg-like. As if this were not enough for native plant lovers, Western Azalea flowers also provide an exciting visual pleasure. The egg-shaped buds are a deep pinkish-red. The 5 petals, fused into a funnel-shaped flower, vary in color from white to light yellow, and are tinged with a delicate pink or orange. The upper lobe of each flower has a yellowish or salmon-colored splotch. The 5 stamens extend 2 to 3 inches beyond the lip of the flower. When in bloom, the flowers—up to 2 inches long—are clustered at the ends of the stems and are so numerous that they almost obscure the foliage. The fruit, a hairy 3/8- to 3/4-inch-long capsule, is woody.

Little documentation of the uses of this plant by Native Californians was found. However, that may not be too surprising given the information listed under "Caution" below.

Western Azalea is one of two *Rhododendron* species native to California. In Greek, "rhodo" means "rosy-colored" and "dendron" means "tree"—a "rosy-colored tree"; *occidentale* means "of the west". Western Azalea is pollinated by hawkmoths that visit in early evening; they are attracted by the light-colored, fragrant flowers.

Western Azalea was discovered by William Lobb, who spent fourteen years collecting seeds for the horticultural firm of Veitch of Exeter, England. It sprouts vigorously following fires or severe pruning.

Caution: All species of this genus contain toxic resins that adversely affect the digestive, cardiac and central nervous systems. The leaves are toxic if ingested, but are not harmful to touch.

94

CALIFORNIA WILD GRAPE

Along a lazy river on a hot, humid summer day, these luxuriant, large-leafed vines—blanketing the treetops or cascading down a canyon wall—remind one of many plants of the south.

Most often you will find California Wild Grape, *Vitis californica*, growing along river banks, near seeps and springs or in damp canyons. It thrives from sea level in the Great Central Valley, up to 3,300 feet in the foothills of the Coast Ranges. It ranges from San Luis Obispo County north to Siskiyou County, and in the Sierra Nevada and the Cascade Range from Kern County north to Shasta County. Forming curtains over the trees or tall shrubs on which it climbs, Wild Grape sometimes covers the plants so thickly that the innocent "props" die for lack of sunlight. It seems to climb most often on the deciduous trees common to stream banks, such as oaks, cottonwoods, alders or maples.

The stems of this woody vine may reach 50 feet in height, climbing skyward with its tendrils. However, without support, it crawls along the ground, on or over rocks or low foliage, forming a small bush only a few feet tall.

Even though the vine dies back to its woody growth each year, the stems can reach several inches in diameter. The stems or "ropes" of Wild Grape, high up in the trees, sometimes provide a natural swing allowing one to glide back and forth across narrow canyons or gullies. But hang on tight!

The young leaves, shoots and branches are covered with dense, white cobwebby hairs. The bark on the stems becomes shreddy with age.

The rich green leaves, nearly round and with scalloped or serrated edges, are 1 1/2 to 5 inches across; the petioles are up to 4 inches long. Arranged alternate on the stem, the leaves are palmately-veined—3 to 5 veins originate from each heart-shaped base. The tendrils—the climbing hooks—and the flower clusters are positioned on the stems in opposition to the leaves. In late fall, the leaves change to various colors: yellow, pink, flame-red or red-purple, depending on each plant's color genes.

Blooming from May to July, the tiny, greenish-yellow, star-like flowers hang from the stems in dense clusters 2 to 6 inches long. Although they are an insignificant visual display, the fragrant blossoms attract many pollinators, especially the bees.

Fruiting in the fall, the wild grapes are smaller and thicker-skinned than table grapes. Unlike the skins of some table grapes, those of the wild grapes slip off easily, separating from the scanty pulp full of pear-shaped seeds. The juicy berries, 1/4 to 1/2 inch round, are covered with bloom—a white waxy or powdery coating found on many native fruits. Sour to taste when eaten fresh, Wild Grapes are also too seedy for most human palates; however, they make an excellent jelly.

Though not a major food source, California Wild Grape was one of eleven species of fruits or berries that were eaten by the northern California natives. The leaves were chewed to quench the thirst; large leaves were used to wrap foods for baking in earthen ovens. Except for the roots, all parts of this plant are edible.

The grape vine was also an emergency water source for the Native Californians. They would climb high in a tree that was supporting the grapevine, then cut off a few of the smaller stems. Back on the ground, they cut the other ends of the same stems and drank the liquid.

Split Wild Grape stems, and sometimes shredded roots, served as twining materials in basket making. Ropes made from Wild Grape stems were indispensable for lashing poles to other materials in the building of granaries and dwellings. The grapes were commonly used as bait when trapping birds and other small animals.

Vitis is the Latin name for the grape vine. The species name, *californica*, means "of California".

TOYON

Tolerating dry summer heat and winter cold, *Heteromeles arbutifolia* is the only plant in its genus found in California. Commonly known as Toyon, it grows in chaparral, oak woodland or mixed evergreen pine forests below 4,000 feet elevation. Toyon is found in the foothills of the Sierra Nevada from Shasta County south to Tulare County and the mountains of southern California. It also grows in the South and North Coast Ranges from Santa Barbara County north through Humboldt County.

An evergreen, tree-like shrub, Toyon reaches up to 15 feet in height, and about half that in width. The bark on its trunk is gray and the young twigs are coated with very fine hairs.

Arranged alternate on the stem, the thick, leathery leaves are oblong to elliptical in shape. With stalks an inch or less long, the leaves are 1 1/2 to 4 inches long and 3/4 to 1 1/2 inches wide. On the top side, the leaves are a shiny, dark-green and the undersides are a dull, paler green. The margins of the leaves are sharply- and regularly-toothed, with a bristly point at each tip.

In June and July, tiny single, rose-like flowers appear in flat-topped clusters at the ends of stems. With 5 petals, the flowers are creamy-white, 3/8 to 1/2 inch across, and have a spicy fragrance that attracts numerous pollinators.

In October, the fruit—a berry-like pome—begins to ripen and changes in color from green to yellow; it turns to reddish-orange by November. The fruits, 1/4 to 1/3 inch in diameter, are persistent and, except for those that the birds eat, remain on the shrub for several months. The mealy pulp of the berries surrounds the 3 to 6 brown seeds.

The Native Californians made considerable use of the Toyon. They prepared a drink from the berries, but the method used is unknown to this author. The berries were almost always processed before being used for food: either by storing them for a couple of months, then roasting them in coals; or by boiling them in water, then baking them in an earthen oven for two or three days. The berries were often eaten with seed meal or pinole. A tea was brewed from the leaves and bark to relieve stomach ailments.

However, the leaves and the seed (or kernel) inside the berries contain cyanogenic compounds and should be considered poisonous. Perhaps the extensive heat processing used by the Native Californians degraded the toxic chemicals, thereby rendering the berries or leaves harmless.

They obtained a tan dye from the berries by simmering them in water.

97

From the Toyon wood, arrows, cooking implements and tools (such as awls, wedges and hide scrapers) were shaped.

Heteromeles means "different apple" from the Greek words "heter" for "different" and "malus" for "apple". *Arbutifolia* means "having foliage like the Arbutus", e.g. with serrated edges. Some other common names include Christmas Berry, California Holly and Hollywood Berry.

Toyon was first collected by Haenke in 1791, probably near Monterey. It was introduced into cultivation by surgeon-naturalist Archibald Menzies in 1796.

Because of excessive commercial harvesting of the berries for holiday decorations, a law was passed in the early 1900s making it illegal to gather Toyon berries. Now there are California state laws protecting all native plants, including the Toyon, on public lands.

Similar to several chaparral plants, Toyon stump-sprouts after fires and helps to stabilize steep slopes following heavy winter rains.

Toyon is one of California's most ornamental shrubs with its dark green holly-like foliage and red berries in winter. (If you'd like to have the berries for decorations, grow your own plant for cuttings. It's not too difficult.)

Caution: The leaves and the seed (or kernel) inside the berries of Toyon contain cyanogenic compounds and should be considered poisonous.

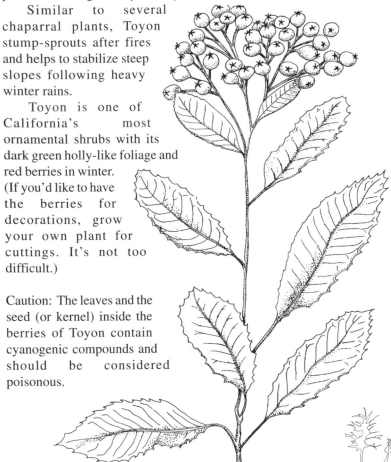

TREE-ANEMONE

In 1846, on his third expedition to the West, General John Fremont discovered *Carpenteria californica* in the Sierra Nevada. He collected a specimen, but failed to document the locality where he found it. (*Carpenteria* is one of two genera Fremont discovered on this trip.)

Carpenteria, or Tree-Anemone, occurs naturally only in scattered colonies in Fresno County, California, and only between the San Joaquin and Kings Rivers from 1,500 to 3,300 feet elevation. Because of its limited natural habitat, it is not surprising that it took several years—until 1875—to be "rediscovered" by Dr. Gustav Eisen, a nurseryman from Fresno.

Found on stream banks or in chaparral or oak woodlands in its native environment, *Carpenteria* is an erect shrub that grows slowly to 10 feet high and 4 to 6 feet wide.

Multi-stemmed from near its base, Tree-Anemone forms a dense bush and its side branches are opposite on the main stem. The light tan bark of the older stems peels off in thin strips; the bark of the young shoots is purplish.

The thick, leathery leaves, arranged opposite on the stem, are a bright dark green and smooth on the upper surface; underneath, they are pale green and covered with short, densely matted, woolly hairs. The oblong evergreen leaves, 1 1/2 to 4 inches long and 1/3 to 1 inch wide, taper at both ends. Generally, the edges of the leaves are rolled under.

A handsome plant the year round, *Carpenteria* is magnificent from June to August when it is decorated with large, white, saucer-shaped flowers, each with a center of over 200 bright yellow stamens.

The flowers are borne either solitarily or in clusters of 3 to 13 at the tips of the erect branches. The 1 1/4- to 2 1/2-inch-wide flowers, with 5 to 8 petals each, emit a delicate, refreshing fragrance, but you must get close to fully enjoy its perfume. The fruit is a conical, leathery capsule about 1/4 to 1/2 inch wide and contains numerous red-brown seeds. This shrub stump-sprouts and can be easily propagated from the many surface suckers.

Carpenteria is one of California's rarest endemic shrubs. Despite its rarity in the wild, *Carpenteria* is often on lists of the ten most attractive native shrubs of California and has been available from the nursery trade since 1908. It is frequently seen in the landscapes of public and private gardens. (There is only one species in this genus.)

The genus was named after Dr. William M. Carpenter, a physician and botanist from Louisiana, who lived from 1811 to 1848. The species name, *californica,* means "of California".

WESTERN LABRADOR TEA

A member of the Heath Family, Western Labrador Tea (*Ledum glandulosum*), prospers in boggy or wet places along the North and Central Coast and in the San Francisco Bay area. Additionally, it is found in the mountains of the North Coast, Klamath and Cascade Ranges and in the Sierra Nevada. Outside of California, it extends north to Canada and east and north to the Rocky Mountains.

Similar to its cousins—the Rhododendrons and Azaleas—Labrador Tea prefers light shade and moisture, thriving in the peaty, acidic soils of wet meadows, marshes and bogs. It may also be found at the spongy edges of mountain lakes and at streamsides. It is a common shrub within its geographic range.

Most often an erect shrub, Labrador Tea may reach up to 5 feet in height. Though the stem bark is smooth, the yellowish-green twigs of this stiffly-branched shrub are generally hairy. Twigs of many of its ground-hugging branches may root where they touch the soil.

When Labrador Tea is out of flower, the leathery leaves remind one of the evergreen Rhododendrons. Clustered near the ends of the branches, the oblong or elliptic leaves are 1/2 to 1 1/2 inches long. Their edges may or may not be slightly rolled under; the leaves are shiny and dark green above, but paler below, with thick white felt-like hairs. Additionally, the lower leaf surface is speckled with resin-dots. (Rhododendrons do not have these resinous glands.)

The leaves, when crushed, exude an odor variously described as similar to turpentine, lemon balm or even strawberries. (Human descriptions of sensations relative to color, odor, taste or touch are subjective, of course, and extremely variable.) It has been reported that the young leaves have a stronger smell than the older ones. Check out the leaves the next time you find the Labrador Tea and draw your own conclusions.

Labrador Tea, with its creamy-yellow to white flowers, blooms from June to August. The blossoms in the flat-topped, 3- to 4-inch-wide clusters are small (less than 1/2 inch wide). Fused only at their bases, each of the 5 petals appears to be separate. The saucer-shaped flowers have 8 to 10 stamens that extend well beyond the petals. The fruit—an elliptical capsule—splits open lengthwise into 5 chambers when dry. Each chamber contains numerous seeds.

The genus name is derived from the Greek word "ledon" for a plant now known as *Cistus* or Rock-Rose. Plants of the genus *Cistus* contain an aromatic resin, the fragrance of which was thought, by some, to be similar to that of the *Ledum* genus. The species name, *glandulosum*, means "full of glands" or "having many glands", a reference to the resin-dots on Labrador Tea's leaves.

There are 2 or 3 species of *Ledum* in the Northern Hemisphere. A handsome shrub, Western Labrador Tea truly reminds one of the high mountains—with blocks of granite, bubbly brooks and wet meadows blanketed with wildflowers. What a sight!

Caution: As is true of many shrubby species in the Heath Family, the entire plant of Labrador Tea, even the nectar, is considered poisonous. Therefore, despite its common name, it should not be used for making any beverages or food.

PEC

MOUNTAIN ASH

Prospering in moist areas of canyons, wooded slopes and coniferous forests, Mountain Ash, (*Sorbus scopulina*), grows between 4,000 and 9,000 feet in elevation. Not a common shrub, Mountain Ash may occasionally be found as a single specimen or with a few of its kind in each location— from Tulare County north to the California-Oregon border in the Sierra Nevada, and in the Cascade, Klamath and North Coast Ranges. An ideal habitat would be amidst the rocks or boulders near a rushing creek— where its feet could find dampness all summer long.

Multi-stemmed, this erect, deciduous shrub is densely branched and is sometimes found in small thickets. Mountain Ash may attain a height of 16 feet, though it more usually is about 10 to 12 feet tall. Its smooth bark is thick and reddish in color, but grays with age.

Each odd-pinnately compound leaf, arranged alternate on the stem, has 9 to 13 oblong-shaped leaflets. The 3/4- to 2 1/2-inch-long leaflets are finely serrated—almost to their wedge-shaped bases. Bright green above, but paler beneath, the smooth leaflets of Mountain Ash are deciduous; in the fall, their color changes to a bright yellow or a brilliant red.

Blooming from June to August, the extravagant Mountain Ash displays as many as 80 to 200 flowers in a 2- to 3-inch flat-topped terminal cluster. Each of the 1/4-inch-wide blossoms with 5 white rounded petals resembles a cherry blossom with its 20 or more yellow stamens.

Each about 1/4 to 1/3 inch in diameter, the coral-red fruits (berry-like pomes borne in huge clusters) decorate the shrub in early fall. Some old-timers harvested the berries after the frosts, believing that the cold reduced the bitter taste of the pulp.

Sometimes, Mountain Ash and Red Elderberry *(Sambucus racemosa* var. *racemosa)* grow side by side and identification of the plants may be difficult. Both have odd-pinnately compound serrated leaflets and a terminal cluster of white flowers.

However, the leaves of Mountain Ash are smooth, bright green in color and arranged alternate on the stem. The leaves of Red Elderberry are larger, not as smooth and a duller green than those of Mountain Ash. In addition, Red Elderberry leaves are arranged opposite on the stems.

The flowers of Mountain Ash, each with 5 sepals and 20 stamens, are borne in flat-topped clusters, while the blossoms of Red Elderberry each have 5 lobed petals fused at their bases and 5 stamens, and are arranged in a pyramidal-shaped cluster. The berries of Mountain Ash are

103

coral-red while those of Red Elderberry are a shiny bright red.

The genus name, *Sorbus*, is the ancient Latin name for this plant. The species name, *scopulina*, a derivative of "scopulis" or "scopulorum" means "rocks" or "of the rocks"—a habitat favored by the Mountain Ash.

As is true with many deciduous plants, Mountain Ash offers change and interest throughout the seasons: the new green leaves in spring, the clusters of white flowers from June to August and the red berries in fall. And, after the yellow or reddish leaves drop in fall, the bare silvery gray branches stand out in the cold of winter. Deciduous plants offer so much visual pleasure if only we stop and look.

DOUGLAS SPIRAEA

Douglas Spiraea grows up to 6,500 feet in elevation in northern California in the north coastal areas, the Inner and Outer North Coast Ranges, the Klamath and Cascade Ranges and the high Sierra Nevada from Butte and Plumas Counties north. Preferring moist, lowland areas and light shade, *Spiraea douglasii*, can be found along stream banks, in swales or near springs in coniferous forests.

An erect shrub, Douglas Spiraea is much larger (3 to 6 feet tall) and has a more open growth habit than Mountain Spiraea. Multi-stemmed, it has many long straight or whip-like ascending branches. New stems are produced from its creeping underground stems, which readily sucker when provided adequate moisture. The bark on the old stems is smooth and reddish brown; on the twigs, it is a pale brown with fine hairs.

The thin leaves of Douglas Spiraea, arranged alternate on the stem, are 1 to 4 3/4 inches long and 1/2 to 1/14 inches wide. They are longer than those of Mountain Spiraea—sometimes up to three times as long. The upper side is green and hairless; underneath, the leaves are matted with dense white hairs. The leaves are one-veined from their bases; their margins are usually serrated above the middle, but sometimes only at the tips. They are more coarsely toothed than those of Mountain Spiraea.

Blooming from June to August, Douglas Spiraea forms 2- to 5-inch pyramidal or spire-like clusters at the ends of the stems. The inflorescence is much taller than it is wide. Another common name, Steeple Bush, could have been suggested by the spire-like shape of the flower sprays. As with Mountain Spiraea, *Spiraea douglasii* has tiny flowers with 5 petals, 5 sepals and countless stamens. The pink stamens extend well beyond the petal tips, and when viewed from a distance, the flower clusters change into soft, wispy, rose-colored plumes.

After blooming, the flower clusters are persistent, remaining on the stems into the winter, but changing color to a rich dark brown. The minuscule fruits, or follicles, are dry and many-seeded.

The genus name, *Spiraea*, is from the Greek word "speira", meaning "band" or "wreath"; it alludes to plants in this genus that were used in garlands. Another common name is Hardhack, whose meaning is unknown. The species name, *douglasii*, refers to David Douglas (1799-1834), a Scottish botanical explorer who discovered the plant.

MOUNTAIN SPIRAEA

Found at a higher elevation than Douglas Spiraea, Mountain Spiraea—a true mountaineer—dwells in the mountains of the Klamath and Cascade Ranges of northern California and in the Sierra Nevada between 2,000 and 11,000 feet in elevation. It prefers moist, rocky areas of the open woods or coniferous forests.

An erect, deciduous shrub up to 3 feet tall, *Spiraea densiflora* has slender stems in dense clumps. The new reddish stems turn gray or brown with age.

Arranged alternate on the stem, the ovate to elliptic leaves vary from 1/2 to 1 1/2 inches long and 1/2 to 3/4 inches wide. Both surfaces of the thin green leaves are hairless or sparsely hairy. One-veined from their rounded bases, the leaves have margins that are toothed from the middle to the leaf tip. They turn a bright yellow in the fall.

Mountain Spiraea blooms in July and August, forming flat-topped clusters 2 to 4 inches wide at the ends of stems. The tiny flower, 1/8 inch across, is rose-like, with 5 petals, 5 sepals and many stamens. The stamens, protruding well beyond the petals, transform the clusters of blossoms into fuzzy puffs of pink. The colorful, fragrant flowers offer a pleasing contrast to the grayish-white granite of the rocky crevices where it often grows.

The fruit, a many-celled dry pod, about 1/8 inch long, breaks open on one side to reveal its dark seeds.

Mountain Spiraea was introduced to Europe in the early 1850s from seed collected by John Jeffrey (1826-1854). He was under contract with the Oregon Association of Scotland to collect plants, especially conifers, in Oregon.

The genus name, *Spiraea*, is from the Greek word "speira", meaning a band or wreath, an allusion to plants in this genus that were used in garlands. The species name, *densiflora*, means "dense-flowered", suggesting many tiny flowers crowded into each cluster (like bees are crowded in a beehive).

Near the babbling creek, with feet still damp from the just melted snow and with fluffy rose clouds floating above bright green leaves, *Spiraea densiflora* announces that spring has arrived in the mountains. Few other shrubs are so bold.

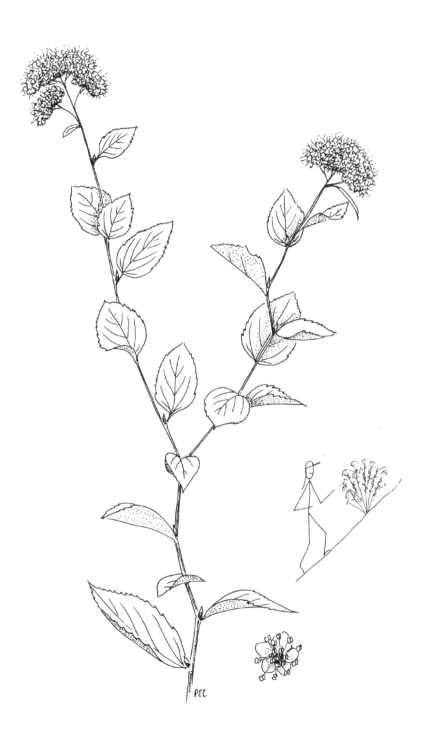

GLOSSARY

Achene. A small dry one-seeded fruit that does not split open at maturity.

Alternate. Leaf arrangement on a stem with only one leaf per node. (See *Illustrations* in the front.)

Anther. The pollen-producing part of the flower situated at the top of the stamen; the male reproductive organ. (See *Illustrations* in the front.)

Axil. The angle formed between a leaf and the stem. (See *Illustrations* in the front.)

Axillary bud. An undeveloped shoot or leaf in the axil at the base of a leaf. (See *Illustrations* in the front.)

Banner. The upright back petal of the Pea or Legume flower.

Berry. A fleshy fruit with seeds mixed throughout the pulp and with no inner core or pit.

Bract. A modified leaf immediately below the solitary flower or the inflorescence.

Burl. A large swelling at the plant's base which connects the outer stems with the inner roots; plants with burls will stump-sprout following fires.

Calyx. The outer or lower ring of flower parts, usually green, that covers the developing bud. (See *Illustrations* in the front.)

Capsule. A dry, many-seeded fruit that splits open on 3 or more sides.

Chaparral. A dense growth of shrubs or small trees usually on hot, dry slopes; common to California.

Circumpolar. Around or near a pole of the earth.

Compound leaf. A leaf that is divided into 2 or more leaflets, the latter having no buds; the leaf may be pinnately or palmately compound. (See *Illustrations* in the front.)

Conifers. Cone-bearing plants, mostly evergreen, with needles or scale-like leaves.

Crown-sprout. See Stump-sprout.

Cyme. A flat-topped inflorescence in which the central flowers bloom first.

Deciduous. Refers to plants that lose all of their leaves at one time and usually only once per year.

Decoction. The solution containing the flavor or essence of plants that is extracted by boiling various plant parts in water.

Dermatitis. An inflammation of the skin that may be caused by contact with some members of the Sumac Family.

Dioecious. Genera that have their reproductive parts, the stamens and pistils, on separate plants.

Diuretic. A medicine or extract of a plant that causes increased urination.

Drupe. A fleshy fruit with a single stone or pit enclosing the seed.

Drupelet. A cluster of many small drupes joined together to form one fruit.

Edgewise. Said of leaves pointing skyward rather than parallel to the ground.

Elliptic(al). Having the shape of an elongated circle; for a leaf, the widest part is in the middle and the leaf tapers to a point at each end.

Endemic. Indigenous; originating in and characterizing a specific region.

Entire. Leaf margins that are continuous and smooth, i.e. without teeth or lobes.

Evergreen. Perennial plants whose leaves remain green throughout the year and are shed intermittently, not all at once.

Family. A broad group of plants, often consisting of several genera, which have similar characteristics based on flower and fruit structures.

Filament. The threadlike structure that supports the anther. (See *Illustrations* in the front.)

Fire drill. A small round stick, often made from California Buckeye, used by the Native Californians when starting fires on wooden, possibly Cedar, hearths.

Follicle. A dry, many-seeded fruit from a simple pistil that splits open along a single line or seam.

Fruit. The dry achene, capsule, follicle or pod, or the fleshy berry, drupe or pome, which contains the mature seeds of a plant.

Funnel-shaped. A flower that is small at its base and gradually widens to its top.

Gall. An abnormal growth or swelling in a plant caused by viral damage, insect egg deposits or chemical irritants, commonly seen on Oak trees and Manzanita leaves.

Genus. The first subdivision of plants in a family that contains related species; the first part of a plant's botanical name. Plural is genera.

Glabrous. Hairless.

Glandular. Bearing glands that often secrete sticky fluids.

Globose. Having a globe shape.

Glutinous. A viscid or sticky secretion.

Great Central Valley or **Great Valley**. The flat interior of California which includes the Sacramento Valley in the north and the San Joaquin Valley to the south; it is approximately 60 miles wide and 400 miles long.

Habitat. The total environment of a plant that supports its specific needs: soil, water, temperature, light, elevation, and companion plants.

Hearth. The woody base, usually made of softer wood than the fire drills, that was used by the native Californians to build fires.

Inflorescence. The entire cluster of flowers on the main flower stem arranged either as heads, umbels, racemes, or panicles.

Infusion. A liquid extract prepared by steeping or soaking the plant parts in water.

Keel. The two fused petals, enclosing the stamens and pistil, located at the base of the Pea or Legume flower.

Lateral leaflets. Side leaflets in a compound leaf.

Leach. To percolate water through a substance to remove unwanted chemicals.

Leaf shapes. (See *Illustrations* in the front.)

Legume. The fruit of the Pea or Legume Family that splits along both sides of the pod.

Lenticels. The openings on the bark of woody twigs that are breathing pores permitting the exchange of oxygen and carbon dioxide between the atmosphere and the inner living tissue.

Lobe. A rounded projection or division as on a leaf.

Lobed. Having lobes extending either halfway to the midrib of the leaf or halfway to the leaf base.

Margin. The edge of a leaf or petal.

Mediterranean-type climate. A climate associated with hot, dry summers and cold, wet winters.

Midrib. The central or middle rib of a leaf.

Montane. Of the mountains.

Multi-stemmed. Plants having more than one stem.

Multi-trunked. Plants having more than one trunk.

Nascent. A term describing the tiny undeveloped inflorescence, common to the Manzanitas, which forms in the fall, but does not mature to full flowering size until spring.

National Formulary. A U.S. governmental agency that publishes official standards for medical drugs with test methods and appropriate dosage. See U.S. Pharmacopeia.

Native Californians. The indigenous people of California who lived here for thousands of years before the arrival of the Europeans.

Nectar. A sugary fluid secreted by some flowers to entice animal pollinators, including moths, bees and butterflies.

Node. The place on a stem from which the leaves or flowers develop. (See *Illustrations* in the front.)

Oblanceolate. A wedge-shaped leaf with a rounded top and ending in a point at the base.

Oblong. A leaf with parallel sides and rounded base and apex.

Obovate. The larger portion of the leaf is near the apex and tapers to a point at the base.

Opposite. The arrangement on a stem of two leaves across from each other at one node, rather than one leaf at each node as is with the alternate leaf arrangement.

Ovary. The seed-producing part of the pistil, situated at the base of the flower. (See *Illustrations* in the front.)

Ovate. Egg-shaped, the widest part of the leaf is near the base.

Palmately compound. A compound leaf with 5 or more leaflets, resembling fingers of the hand, which originate from one point at the tip of the petiole. (See *Illustrations* in the front.)

Palmately lobed. A simple leaf with 5 or more deeply cut lobes. (See *Illustrations* in the front.)

Palmately-veined. A simple leaf with 5 or more veins arising from the base of the leaf.

Panicle. A compound raceme; a diversely branching flower cluster. (See *Illustrations* in the front.)

Pedicel. The stalk of an individual flower in an inflorescence.

Peduncle. The main flower stalk of a solitary flower or of an entire inflorescence.

Pemmican. A nourishing food made from dried fruit (berries, currants, cherries or plums) mixed with meat or fish and animal fat. Formed into cakes, it was an easy-to-carry high calorie food for travel.

Persistent. Refers to the inflorescence, fruit or leaves of deciduous plants (such as Spicebush or Spiraeas) that dry up, yet remain on the plant into the winter.

Petals. The showy, colored parts of a flower, though sometimes bracts or sepals take over that function. (See *Illustrations* in the front.)

Petiole. The stalk that attaches a leaf to the stem. Leaves having stems are described as petioled.

Pinnately compound. A compound leaf whose leaflets are arranged opposite on the stem (the rachis) and which has no terminal leaflet. (See *Illustrations* in the front.)

Pinnately compound, odd-. A compound leaf whose leaflets are arranged opposite on the stem (the rachis) and which has a terminal leaflet. (See *Illustrations* in the front.)

Pinnately lobed. A simple leaf with deeply cut lobes along each side of the midrib or rachis.

Pinole. A meal or flour made from small seeds that were parched, then pulverized and eaten. At times, the pulverized seeds were made into cakes.

Pistil. The seed producing organ of the flower consisting of the stigma, style and ovary; one flower may have one to many pistils. (See *Illustrations* in the front.)

Pith. The soft spongy tissue in the center of a stem.

Plumose. Similar in shape or appearance to a feather.

Pod. The dry fruit of the Pea or Legume Family that splits along two edges.

Pollen. Fine, dust-like substance found in the anthers; each grain contains two cells that divide to form the male sperm cells.

Pome. A fleshy fruit, resembling an apple, with seeds enclosed in an inner core.

Poultice. A soft mass of herbs or meal, wrapped in cloth or large leaves, which was applied hot to parts of the body as a remedy for various ills; a hot pad of early times.

Prickle. A small sharp thorn or projection on a plant.

Purgative. Medicine or herbs that cause cleansing of the gastro-intestinal tract.

Raceme. An unbranched inflorescence in which the flowers—opening from bottom to top—are borne on short stalks along the main stem.

Rachis. The midrib of a pinnately lobed or pinnately compound leaf.

Receptacle. The bottom or platter on which the parts of the flower rest.

Rhizome. An underground stem, growing horizontally, that roots on its underside.

Scrub. A large area covered with low trees and shrubs.

Sepal. One individual part of the outer ring of a flower that is usually green. (See *Illustrations* in the front.)

Serrate. Having teeth pointing toward the apex of a leaf, not outward.

Sessile. A leaf or flower attached to the main stem without a stalk (such as a petiole, peduncle or pedicel).

Simple leaf. An undivided single leaf blade (which may be lobed or have an irregular margin); having no leaflets.

Species. A division of members of a genus into groups of plants that share common characteristics and also interbreed freely; the second part of a botanical name.

Spike. An unbranched inflorescence, the flowers of which are attached to the stem without pedicels.

Spine. A sharp-pointed outgrowth, occurring at the nodes, which is derived and modified from a leaf.

Stamen. The pollen-bearing organ of a flower, consisting of the filament and the anthers.

Stem. The stalk of a plant that supports the leaf, flower or fruit.

Stigma. The part of a pistil that receives the pollen. (See *Illustrations* in the front.)

Stump-sprout. The resumption of plant growth (the sending forth of new shoots) after fire or severe pruning.

Style. Part of the pistil, a narrow round stalk that connects the ovary to the stigma. (See *Illustrations* in the front.)

Tendril. Threadlike, modified leaf parts or petioles of climbing plants which coil or spiral around other plants or structures for support.

Terminal. At the end, such as a terminal leaflet or bud.

Thicket. A dense growth of shrubs or small trees, almost impenetrable to humans without some thinning; a veritable haven for numerous animals.

Toothed. Having tooth-like indentations along the leaf edge, pointing out, not up toward apex; dentate. (See *Illustrations* in the front.)

Trumpet-shaped. A cone-shaped flower, small at its base and widely flared at its tip.

Tubular. A flower with regular-shaped petals that are united at the base to form a tube.

Twice or thrice pinnately compound. A situation in which each leaflet of the compound leaflet is further divided into leaflets. (See *Illustrations* in the front.)

Umbel. A head of flowers whose stems or pedicels branch out from the same point of the main flower stem or peduncle in an umbrella- or spoke-like fashion. (See *Illustrations* in the front.)

Unarmed. Without thorns or spines.

Urushiol. The chemical irritant in Poison Oak that may produce a skin rash following exposure.

U.S. Pharmacopeia. A U.S. governmental agency that publishes a list of medicinal drugs, their formulas and methods for synthesizing or extracting the useful components.

Viscid. Sticky (or viscous) on the surface.

Willow-shaped. A narrow leaf up to 4 times as long as wide and tapering to a point at each end.

SELECTED BIBLIOGRAPHY

Balls, Edward K. 1962. *Early Uses of California Plants*, California Natural History Guides: 10. Berkeley and Los Angeles: University of California Press.

Barbour, Michael, Bruce Pavlik, Frank Drysdale, and Susan Lindstrom. 1993. *California's Changing Landscapes: Diversity and Conservation of California Vegetation*. Sacramento, CA: The California Native Plant Society.

Barrett, Samuel A. and Edward W. Gifford. 1933. *Miwok Material Culture: Indian Life of the Yosemite Region*. Bulletin of Milwaukee Public Museum, Vol. 2, No. 4. Yosemite National Park, CA: Yosemite Association.

Blackwell, Laird R. 2002. *Wildflowers of the Eastern Sierra and Adjoining Mojave Desert and Great Basin*. Renton, WA: Lone Pine Publishing.

Casebeer, MaryRuth. 1999. With Eyes of Wonder Series, Vol. 1, *Discover California Wildflowers*. Sonora, CA: Hooker Press.

Clarke, Charlotte Bringle. 1977. *Edible and Useful Plants of California*, California Natural History Guides: 41. Berkeley and Los Angeles: University of California Press.

Clements, Edith S. 1928. *Flowers of Coast and Sierra*. New York: The H. W. Wilson Company.

Coate, Barrie D. 1980. *Selected California Native Plants in Color*. Saratoga, CA: Saratoga Horticultural Foundation.

Coats, Alice M. 1969. *The Plant Hunters*. New York: McGraw-Hill Book Company.

Coffey, Timothy. 1993. *The History and Folklore of North American Wildflowers*. New York: Houghton Mifflin Company.

Coombes, Allen J. 1994. *Dictionary of Plant Names*. Portland, OR: Timber Press, Inc.

Cornell, Ralph Dalton. 1978, rev. ed. *Conspicuous California Plants: With Notes on Their Garden Uses*. Los Angeles: The Plantin Press.

Dale, Nancy. 1986. *Flowering Plants, the Santa Monica Mountains, Coastal and Chaparral Regions of Southern California*. Santa Barbara, CA: Capra Press.

Day, Sara. 1992. *A Collection of U.S. Commemorative Stamps*. N.p.: United States Postal Service.

Elmore, Francis H. 1976. *Shrubs and Trees of the Southwest Uplands*, Popular Series No. 19. Tucson, AZ: Southwest Parks and Monuments Association.

Ferris, Roxana S. 1968. *Native Shrubs of the San Francisco Bay Region*, California Natural History Guides: 24. Berkeley and Los Angeles: University of California Press.

Fuller, Thomas C. and Elizabeth McClintock. 1986. *Poisonous Plants of California*, California Natural History Guides: 53. Berkeley and Los Angeles: University of California Press.

Hall, Clarence A., Jr., Ed. 1991. *Natural History of the White-Inyo Range, Eastern California*, California Natural History Guides: 55. Berkeley and Los Angeles: University of California Press.

Haskin, Leslie Loren. 1934. *Wild Flowers of the Pacific Coast*. Portland, OR: Metropolitan Press.

Hickman, James C., Ed. 1993. *The Jepson Manual: Higher Plants of California*. Berkeley and Los Angeles: University of California Press.

James, Wilma Roberts. 1973. *Know Your Poisonous Plants*. Healdsburg, CA: Naturegraph Publishers.

Jepson, Willis Linn. 1923, 2nd ed. *The Trees of California*. Berkeley, CA: Associated Students Store, University of California.

Johnston, Verna R. 1994. *California Forests and Woodlands: A Natural History*, California Natural History Guides: 58. Berkeley and Los Angeles: University of California Press.

Keator, Glenn. 1994. *Complete Garden Guide to the Native Shrubs of California*. San Francisco, CA: Chronicle Books.

——. 1994. *Plants of the East Bay Parks*. Niwot, CO: Roberts Rinehart Publishers, Inc.

Kruckeberg, Arthur R. 1982. *Gardening with Native Plants of the Pacific Northwest: An Illustrated Guide*. Seattle and London: University of Washington Press.

Labadie, Emile L. 1978. *Native Plants for Use in the California Landscape*. Sierra City, CA: Sierra City Press.

Lenz, Lee W. 1956. *Native Plants for California Gardens*. Claremont, CA: Rancho Santa Ana Botanic Garden.

Lloyd, Francis E. and Beverly Hackett. 1973. *Flowers of the Foothills: An Introduction to 81 California Wildflowers*. Truckee, CA: Tulip Press.

McMinn, Howard E. 1939. *An Illustrated Manual of California Shrubs*. Berkeley and Los Angeles: University of California Press.

Morgenson, Dana C. 1975. *Yosemite Wildflower Trails*. El Portal, CA: Yosemite Natural History Association.

Munz, Philip A. 1961. *California Spring Wildflowers*. Berkeley and Los Angeles: University of California Press.

——. 2003, rev. ed. *Introduction to California Mountain Wildflowers*, California Natural History Guides: 68. Berkeley and Los Angeles: University of California Press.

Murphey, Edith Van Allen. 1959. *Indian Uses of Native Plants*. Ukiah, CA: Mendocino County Historical Society.

Parsons, Mary Elizabeth. 1909. *The Wild Flowers of California*. San Francisco, CA: Cunningham, Curtiss & Welch.

Rice, Bertha M. and Roland Rice. 1920. *Popular Studies of California Wild Flowers*. San Francisco, CA: Upton Bros. and Delzella Publishers.

Schmidt, Marjorie G. 1980. *Growing California Native Plants*, California Natural History Guides: 45. Berkeley and Los Angeles: University of California Press.

Spellenberg, Richard. 1979. *The Audubon Society Field Guide to North American Wildflowers: Western Region.* New York: Alfred A. Knopf, Inc.

Stearn, William T. 1983, 3rd ed., rev. *Botanical Latin.* North Pomfret, VT: David & Charles, Inc.

Storer, Tracy I. and Robert L. Usinger. 1963. *Sierra Nevada Natural History: An Illustrated Handbook.* Berkeley and Los Angeles: University of California Press.

Strike, Sandra S. 1994. *Ethnobotany of the California Indians,* Vol. 2: *Aboriginal Uses of California's Indigenous Plants.* Champaign, IL: Koeltz Scientific Books USA.

Stuart, John D. and John O. Sawyer. 2001. *Trees and Shrubs of California,* California Natural History Guides: 62. Berkeley and Los Angeles: University of California Press.

Sweet, Muriel. 1976. *Common Edible and Useful Plants of the West.* Healdsburg, CA: Naturegraph Publishers, Inc.

Tadd, Brown. 1988. *One Miwok's View of Native Food Preparations and the Medicinal Uses of Plants.* N.p.: Three Forests Interpretive Association.

Thomas, John Hunter and Dennis R. Parnell. 1974. *Native Shrubs of the Sierra Nevada.* California Natural History Guides: 34. Berkeley and Los Angeles: University of California Press.

Thompson, Steven and Mary Thompson. 1976, rev ed. *Wild Food Plants of the Sierra.* Berkeley, CA: Wilderness Press.

Weeden, Norman F. 1996, 4th ed. *A Sierra Nevada Flora.* Berkeley, CA: Wilderness Press.

Whitney, Stephen. 1985. *Western Forests.* National Audubon Society Nature Guides. New York: Alfred A. Knopf, Inc.

Wilson, Lynn, Jim Wilson and Jeff Nicholas. 1990. *Wildflowers of Yosemite.* El Portal, CA: Sierra Press, Inc.

116

INDEX of PLANT NAMES

117

For more copies of *Discover California Shrubs* or *Discover California Wildflowers:*

Check out your Local Bookstore – or
Call toll-free 1-800-696-5997 to place an order with Hooker Press – or
Order by mail using the form below

ORDER FORM

Name: _____

Billing Address: _____

City, State, Zip Code: _____

Shipping Address (if different than above):

Name: _____

Street: _____

City, State, Zip Code: _____

Item *Quantity*   *Price*

Discover California Shrubs   _____ x $17.95 = $_____

Discover California Wildflowers   _____ x $14.95 = $_____

Add shipping: Shipping $_____
   For one book, add $4.00
   For each additional book sent to the
     same address, add $2.00
   For each additional shipping address,
     attach address & order information;
     for one book, add $4.00
     for each additional book sent to
     same shipping address, add $2.00
                 TOTAL $_____

Enclose check or money order made payable to Hooker Press and send to:

Hooker Press
P.O. Box 3957
Sonora, CA 95370-3957